Copyright © 2018 by Macheté

All rights reserved. This collection and any portion thereof can only be reproduced or altered by the author and or publisher. No other man, woman, child, person, agency, corporation, entity or agent thereof may reproduce this collection or any portion thereof without the sole express written permission being granted by the author or publisher.

Any and all fraudulent act(s) conspired, committed or attempted against the author and or publisher, regarding this collection are punishable under, but not limited to:
18 USC § 1001(a)(1)(2)

***To prevent the event of theft -- *Fair, but minimal and in part, use of this collection is allowed under 17 U.S. Code § 107*

***For any questions or anything else, please feel free to contact me:

delanochearts@outlook.com

Special thanks to:
Amber Lee Jones

She is the sole creative professional *artista* behind the artwork you see on the front and back cover of this book, and/or anywhere else you see it.

The ideas, imageries and layouts I pitched to her though my lil' basic sketches were easy for her to grasp and bring to life. I must say that, she is quite the professional in her ethics. Her helping me with this work is unexplainable and I seriously thank her for her time.

Ms. Williams is open to contact for business.

She can be reached at:

<u>sofritojones@gmail.com</u>

graciaaaaaaaaasss!!!

Food for thought...

If you saw yourself in your front yard, would you recognize yourself? From my experiences and interactions with many people throughout my life, I can see that most people have no idea about who and what they are: they do NOT recognize themselves. It is not for me to tell why they don't, but it is pertinent that you to recognize yourself. Opinions other than that of yourself do not matter. At least try to know yourself, why the fuck not?

Think about that for a while, in complete silence...

...Did you hear anything?

...O' well...

It's time to read...

For me myself;
and Abuela

Macheté, conceptualized

  Stemming from the end of the first volume of *Conversational Topography,* and being a continuation of the collection, *The Book of Macheté* is a world of its own, brought to life through the enhanced wordplay and mechanical illustrations of an original man who loves pencils and pens.
  There will be no types of bafoonery in this volume - none at all. From cover to cover, I attempted to let a little of my internal fire extend itself from my heart onto paper via words; everything I present to you is real and I must say that there are no boundaries in this book. The poetic work here is quite extensive, which provides the reader with an abundance of poetry to peel through and bookmark, reference, favor, dislike, etc; whereas the first book, *From Me to You,* may not have provided the reader with the opportunity to do such things. In addition to more poetry, there are also a few short stories that are embers of another fire in my vast world which are now included in this book. I must present myself as a writer, an artist; so here – I give you thought again, in a second volume.

I, Macheté, am not a part of any group or group think tank, party, affiliation, agency, "anything you have studied or came across on social media through propaganda and sensationalism," **none of that.** Ain't no panel of niggas nowhere in my life; I wrote every single word in/of this book all by myself, and may you read in good spirits. I didn't go super miles deep with the *etymon,* but I went deep enough; you'll see it. As far as my *spanish (e.g. ancient latin, south-american, central-american, mexican-american "languages")* I wrote it mostly off the top of my head to see what I can do; hence, I didn't do long hours of editing out of respect of the language, although I did study some too; plus, I just like the language, always have. I think I'm good at it to be honest, but I need work - It'll come.

This collection consists of *raw* poetry composed and compiled from at least the years of 2014-2018, respectively; the short stories where created latter 2017-2018, respectively. What I write is what I think; filtered from the sights in my eyes that are layered in my brain- written to the, almost, well...a little to the best of my ability without overdoing things.

Skin color plays not a factor in my standard observations. Many people have personally seen to it to bring detriment to my life, and there's nothing I can about it. Instead of waring with and destroying these uninheritable persons, which would cause additional stress on my life, I choose to always destroy you with my words and almighty pen.

I *destroy* you. *You are destroyed.*

La tabla de materias

For...	*ix*
Macheté, conceptualized.	x
La tabla de materias	15

Capitulo Uno — 25

Immemorial	27
Excerpt for like minds	28
The Introduction	30
Ya' don't say	31
A little more Macheté	32
Finding my own beat	33
Wall of Art	34
Warrior of me	35
Prelude to Reconnaissance	36
Flirting with the lady in red	37
¿Dónde es Utopia?	38
Lazy ethics	39
Gon' somewhere	40
Freeze	41
They just can't keep up	42
The Defiant	43
Why tho'?	44
Compromised by a catch 22	45

The water was so high	46
A feeling, so to speak	47
A brief overview	48
Life is not fair	49
Check this out tho'	50
Welcome to weird	53
Illusions of Grandeur	54
Programming	55
Without much thought	56
Listen to me	57
I don't want it	59
Blanks to fill	60
Play with them not me	61
We all have rough nights	62
Me against me	64
Early days for me	66
It's dark out here	68
Grow up	69
A rally cry	70
Another poem before bed	71
Early days for me, 2	72
Plural reception	73
The bright of dark	74
I'll get you	75
Mind games as I age	76
Poetic wordplay	78
Circle of sand, quick	79
Words from my pineal	81

Cemetary at dark	83
Macheta	85
Where art thou?	86
Don't play games	87
Short Story: Fetch	**89**

Capitulo dos — *108*

The pathway of Macheté	110
The Marksmanship of a pen	111
A slight breeze	112
Where darkness fell	113
I'm getting tired	115
Night fuel, brief	116
Colón would say	117
Purposeless MF's	118
The Game	120
Questions, 2	121
De la noche, a brief	122
Fuck Friendz	123
I am not your friend	124
What time is it?	125
Random Poetic Violence	126
Before or after	127
Macheté wept	128
From a certain standpoint	129
Fuego	130
Drop you off in Iceland	131

Canister of air	132
The contagion	133
Being me myself	134
Before a napmare	135
Cranberries for everyone	136
A christmas carol!!!	137
Recruiting, a de la noche sonnet	138
Archery	140
De facto	141
…Just am	142
To the elders	143
Inertia	144
Nothing but wordplay, that's all	145
A question for…who?	146
Hello; Biatch	147
Free Lunch!!!	148
Life has no script	149
"The heat, the heat"	150
! Don't do it Macheté!	151
The codex	152
The missings	153
Approxiamately	154
Astral Plane	155
The Heat, again	157
Vitality Molecules	158
Why won't they?	159
They tryna' give me the black plague man!	160
A statement	161

A different start, but worthy…LOL	162
Announcement 1	163
Short story: Who was I talking to?	**165**
<u>Capitulo tres</u>	**185**
A Mad society	187
What guns are for	188
The sadness	189
The end of the beginning	190
The beginning of the end	191
¡¡¡Cuidadooo!!!	192
Partials from Macheté	193
Pick this apart	194
These people are real Pokemón	195
By 2	196
Minescules	197
Macheté, the beauty of it all	198
Pendejos	199
Don't include them	200
¡¡¡Pistolas!!!	201
I drink blood	202
De la noche, again bitch	203
Show me watcha' got	205
(your title goes here)	206
El invierno dos veces	207
En mí palabras	208
My disclosure	209

Fear of the Unknown	210
No authenticas	211
How is this?	212
Grafted Explosion	213
Before Bed 2014	214
Hoy es hace calor	215
Bad weather	216
Beneath State	217
¿Donde estoy?	218
Regurgitation	219
What's up???	220
¿ Quien es en?	221
Galaxies baby, galaxies	222
The last full moon!!!	223
4 minutes	224
9 minutes	225
What is up?	226
I just don't know why	227
Running on	228
En Sanguine	229
Last quarter of 2016	230
Halloween, a de la noche story	231
Intrusion	232
Oye!	233
Who in the world are you people?	234
Eyes on the stars	235
The riddler	236
Elegant Acts	237

Brazen Scientifics	238
The wrong ones	239
You should just keep walking	240
Short Story:	
It just happened so fast	243

Ending Pieces...   **261**

i

Immemorial

How is it that
the black sheep of the family
is the main one to
visit grandmas' grave?

Nobody knows, and not even me -
at times,
of me I think less -
never will I know why they don't see her.

As I cold am, my youth was hateful -
aged and viced - that more than life.
As I cold am, I visit grandmas' grave -
no matter what time no matter what day.

One fall night, I stopped by her grave -
drugged as norm, drove straight to the grave.
Walked to her site to let words out,
gun in hand in case fate came out.

As I cold am, I visit grandma's grave -
no matter what time no matter what day.

Excerpt for like minds

Dark night, dark night - into thee I flee,
down a lone path mapping my first graph.
Since it's mine now the lone map is blank -
ready for me to rename everything.
Not only land but bodies of water,
of this new map I'm solely the scholar.

Dark night, dark night - within thee I flee,
nowhere can I go but to my destiny!
Sharpening knives and polishing swords,
stockpiling truth and firming accords
of standing on two about my name,
watching my brain to free its birth.

Not do I choose to harm at all,
they who fake they shall not get.
Growing my line I won't shed blood...

work draws blood I must draw first –

far from perfect still planting my trees ---
dark night, dark night -
into thee I flee.

The Introduction

The flood gates are now open,
in the wash comes Macheté
sharp with an old tongue,
direct and steady.

Ya' don't say

Fruiting from water as the
universal solvent
is whole man,
it's best to drink the water.
Deep are the thoughts -- on fire is the soul
of this heartbeat, steady like a sniper's scope.
Out of the earth tone all year though
is one small man large enough to love home.

Fuck this world of media tricks,
in comes truth leaving thieves speechless.
Rock is the truth and is solely innate,
sure with a need of breathing in shape.
Livin' like this is just to leave a
metamorphic race
of colder souls within their fate ---

Ignited is igneous fire of earth.

A little more Macheté

Macheté will do what some won't do -
slit your fuckin' throat and
send you back to school
with an open wound,
flood the class with salt...
tell teach' I said fuck you and them too.

I'm foolish to you?
My kindness is weakness?
Now...
...I flood your land with the
strongest bleach,
tainting taste in the food you eat.

Finding my own beat

In a
room full of silence is how you find your beat,
spruce it,
box it --
mail to self promptly.

Wall of Art

Life is live action without one pause,
inscribed as a no wash cloth free for all.
New at the time of the first heartbeat,
blacking out short when the beings' eyes blink.
Seconds of life are closely recorded
inside of the brain, a part of your frame.
In still-life style, and able to be drawn -
life is personified as an art form,
moving by play or in rhythm with wind -
written on paper, etched in print -
spoken in circles of women and men

bating a date for when they will care.

Life may slow, never is it late,
speeds up a hint once the soul leaves face.

Forever life flows, pushing past the gates
into stargates –
dumping in galactic lakes.

Warrior of me

Drilling for oil,
searching for slaves -
setting up traps,
placing the bait.
Mining the troves
pocketing gold,
mapping all routes
finding things out.
Stockpiling truth
sugars and fruits,
loving the land
crops by hand,
studying life
enjoying grand,
one edge for flight -
ready to fan.

Prelude to Reconnaissance

"If naked and afraid mixes with the walking dead, here you see clones and mutes walking naked…"

Flirting with the lay in red

She walks fast and talks even faster,

in the form of a
solid silk red dress.

Foots in cars of men slow down,
those who past can briefly bask...

Lady is tense, rips through a fence -
face of mad grandma with a switch.

Going to win at speeds of trains she
uses wind through drops of rain -
not one spot on that red dress.
He who wants knows of her test,
and her scent when in the street -
seek calmly, she can't be beat.

¿Donde es Utopia?
Un cancion

Utopia es en su cabeza,
en su vida, en su cama,
con abuela, con abuelo,
con mama, con papa,
con hermana, con hermano,
con hija, con hijo,
con nieta, con nieto,
con sobrina, con sobrino,
con cuñada, con cuñado.
Si ninguno de eso,
entonces contigo.

Utopia es con muchas cosas,
o Utopia es contigo.

Lazy Ethics

Workin' for a goal,
working just to save,
all around will share
if it's all the same -
working just the same
if not very close,
those who choose to wait
causing things to slow,
when the prize is here
it they will not hold.

Gon' somewhere

Can't pay me off so you
play sandbox and dirt
my road with chicken pox-
...bringin' me an itch that
I need to scratch-
code words passed to
stab me in the back.

Freeze

Go as you please but spare me mine,
much is gone away so I lack spare time.
Gone with the thief and stuck with thief
is a strawman that they made out of me.

They just can't keep up

If it ain't about weave-
new shoes or
tv,
a song full of mumbles,
church and its cheese,
being black slaves or
pills and fake weed-
lust for a car that
came from overseas,
a false love life and
weak family tree-
sloppy drug deals but
never ran the street...

nobody cares but black
lives matter?

Leavin' momma last just
because she's not lit,
the joke is on you and
you will be fixed.

The Defiant

How is my life in the
hands of another,
playing a part of
what goes in the cupboard...

...can't do this forever

Why tho'

Why tho,
hate the lady with the afro?
That came down from the sky tho?

Compromised by a catch 22
From the desk of a real European

Tell us that you're black by checking that line and we'll smooth play it off like we care but we swear to Vicar that we don't, though we know you didn't get to what you call home on a boat, you were already here and that's for us to know. All we do best is lie in your face about the place you didn't come from 'cause we're sure you'll believe us but won't believe your mom nor grandma because you're dumb from our allocated propaganda scum that has tainted your blood for centuries to come. Over the course of so many years we've taken your land by so many tears that we didn't shed but all your people did, some of those same people helped us do you in, then we turned around and did them in; we play intricate.

Thank you

The water was so high

The rolling tide of mud from the last great flood was increased by the blood of the great young men of copper no tan that were buried in the mud. No one cares but the men with a heart like a woman with a lioness stare, a lioness grip of lioness fair; woven to live and won't sit around and stare, will lend a helping hand to the hurt man.

A feeling, so to speak

Fuck a dict Arnold, and the followers,
head shots at all until blood spills.
Group 'em in a net, take jaws of life
and claw their insides until hollow -
sorrow plays a part not
when throwing darts at Arnold -
therefore,
bring the pain and never any sorrow.

This bitch dict wouldn't slay with the rest,
ran to the other team,
spilled the beans to the chests.

A brief overview

maniac hands of manual labor
at the forefront moving to the homefront
checking my pulse to see if I died
heavily slum it shows in my eyes ---

eradicating all denying my claim
to anything on earth anything I crave
evaporating death irrigated to me
using my blood to water my sea

Life is not fair

The fairest of all is not really fair,
truly is rude if not in her realm,
treating the people as servants at least,
ranking a beauty the same as a beast
unless that beauty is somewhat like she,
brittle with caring for any beneath
the status of those who alter the streets,
allocates taxes and alters the beats
deep in the hearts who work hard just to eat,
hard just to eat, hard just to eat!

The fairest of all is wrong for a heal,
not like an addict who looks for a deal -
more like a queen in a queendom of serfs,
only cordial if it quenches her thirst.

The fairest of all is not always fair -
the holder of cards does not always play
unless it can net a golden walkway -
free of debris that is cramping her air,
moving with feeling that no one is there,
basking in nothing but cancerous sweets
to sour the hearts who work hard just to eat -
hard just to eat, hard just to eat!

The fairest of all is not always fair.

Check this out tho'

Somewhere in the abyss is hell,
lonesome,
quiet,
all by itself --
hungry for blood, waiting for help
to drink the blood of Loki's belt.

Is hell somewhere in the abyss?
Sad as a dog without a bone,
bored as women who seldom moan,
groaning because it has no home;
if good souls die, hell will not know.
Lucifer has to ring its bell.

Hell is somewhere in the abyss,
nothing and no one to play with.
Hell is a gnat who wears black slacks -
or a thin skirt that is red and black,
wearing no top to show its back,
showing its chest, hopes to attract.
Shoes are loaf like cleats for the tracks
that follow the weak souls who may crack.

Somewhere in hell is the abyss,
with a face stuck in old world myth.
For its age not looking too sick,

pretty and fine with youthfulness;
handsome with new youthfulness.
Hunting for souls to bring them here ---
swinging its hair, hell hath no fear.
Fists of fate --- its hellish grip,
long down the back is hells hair reel,
hunting for souls to bring them here.

Somewhere is the abyss in hell,
all it can eat are weak humans
who think at heart that hell exists,
thinking on hell all day stasis -
much they live through life hellbent,
spawning themselves in hellishness
drenched in slime in hell's outfit
riding themselves of heavens' scent,
eating a path of concrete bricks -
left with teeth of broken sticks.

In hell somewhere is the abyss,
meaningless and broken in six
divided by three - two options
at least- die now or die soon!
Take a drink from that red lagoon
that stews the men to be consumed.
Inhale a scent of souls that brew
behind the scenes like old cartoons.

In the abyss somewhere is hell,
inside its shell ringing its bell,

harnessing cells to cast its spell
on those who gave up how they felt
about the scent of heavens' belt -
ashamed inside but who to tell?

Somewhere in the abyss is hell -
lonesome,
quiet -
all by itself;
hungry for blood, waiting for help
to drink the blood of Loki' belt.

Welcome to weird

Where art thou sun moon?
You used to be
on my left eyebrow,
standing on my arch
as a cash cow.
Helping me to watch
for deads if alive ---
I extract my insides and
hummm high by a fire,
grouping the thick fumes
from my past life then
bagging my past,
blowing breath on it thrice.

The fire has grown
from wind came ice,
my own tornado
granulated my life!

Where art thou sun moon?
You used to be so serene,
posted on my eyebrow
like an antebellum army -
steady in your pairing
for anyone to fit me,
any young lady

who won't bring scarring -
can send a hint without
hashtagging something -
you used to help me out,
now I start with nothing.

Where are thou sun moon?
Did my welcome overstay?
Or did something change your mood?

Illusions of Grandeur

When it comes the time to show watcha' got,
some catch a snag and begin to detract-
claimin' all the sayin's that sound so sweet,
when the heat comes and pheromones secrete
all the truth shows who really made the beat-
wrote the whole song before they went to sleep
he you will see is the face of the team
standing in the shadows – other folks lean,
never did they think the truth they will see-
all has came to light, now I really see.

Programming

Thick yarn thin eye,
are you choking yet?
Breath by breath do you fall a step,
not with the flu but
sick of yourself.

Without much thought

Innerself mindset all day no stress,
rights to wrongs surely won't get left
out in the sun to bake with the rest,
those who resolve to slip from the breast
of she who carried you loved you best,
fell into the wrong hands lost respect-
life ahead of you won't be the best,
yea you made fiat but wore a dress
wore some lipstick on your lips and chest,
to the real people you are a pest.

Listen to me

I'm not a kind of man,
      but man do I be-
I'm not a ceiling fan,
      but through wind I see-
I'm not somebody's friend,
      but whole do I be-
I'm not to always trust,
      but I won't be green-
I'm not too much in love,
      but I soon will be.

I'm no from Africa,
      but you think I am-
I'm not a color code,
      but you say I am-
I'm not a silly boy,
      but you claim I am.

I'm not american???
      But my roots are here...

I don't want it

Your apples are poison your thoughts the same-
scribbled my history and called it plain,
all that you have it was stolen from me-
saw you from land so we hid in the trees,
docking your ships in the land of the free-
land of the fruits and the berries indeed,
into our land and its glorious scene,
looking for something you read in your scheme-
read from a journal of previous thieves
looking for souls to inject your disease.

Blanks to fill

The money is yours
      so is the debt,
many forsaken to drink from the rest,
milking resources to hide from the rest-
which are the workers that buildeth the best,
watering land recycleth best
warming the land with the beats from their chests,
without these souls you would fall to your death.

Play with them, not me

You keep
that bible under
your pillow but you
lie to the people who
pass around the
plate and pay your
way to live fake.

How dare you
claim to love *god* but
you are the
devil-
no disguise no ties
to tell the truth you rather not,
overnight,
you will lose
everything you got.

We all have rough nights

Dark night, dark night; I see you again!
This time you don't seem happy,
what happened to your grin?
Last I saw of you, we were best friends -
this time you seem upset,
I see some life within.

Dark night, dark night; you never deal with light,
did something infiltrate?
What happened to your might?
When the days change are you not dark night?
Hope you live forever -
if not that won't be right.

Dark night, dark night, you seem a little sick,
I can see your cauldron,
where is your wooden stick?
If you lose your skin are you on death's bed?
Is a darker shadow
en route to fill you in?

Dark night, dark night - how do we fix your soul?
How is it you got hurt,
when nothing can get close -
even your favorite ghosts,
to nothing on your turf?

Somewhere a culprit lurks.

Dark night, dark night - I truly have to go,
just came by to visit,
because you didn't show
at my favorite show, nor
did your mate. I'm alone
now, in my favorite zone,
laying by a fire
burning from a stone,
staring at the twilight
to conjure up my drone.

Dark night, dark night, next time you better show!

Me against me

Beyond my widows' peak is the darkness of me,
not a third eye but an eye of mystique.
Close to the size of oceanic bodies
is the moat surrounding my castle of a brain.
Eye of mystique is deep and opaque,
aiming to taint my pineal lake.

This dark in me is deep inside,
tuned to nature, much open to evil.
Built on my castle are protons for weapons,
neutrons for bricks, won't find electrons -
'less you dig deep for my magical wand.
Eye of mystique won't do well in the sun,
falls upon me when it senses a hole -
tries to patch me with the seed of control
to rebuild me as a body of null -
sad and unable to patch that hole.

Beyond my widows' peak is the darkness of me,
not a third eye but an eye of mystique.
In a rowboat with a paddle of lashes
used as a filter to fight all the traps
that serve as a barter to thicken the moat
that causes my castle not to be encroached,
not by a spider nor by its approach.
Eye of mystique must sit still or die off,
invading my castle is one of its goals -

be as I think - it won't get close,
blinking fatigue as it wades in the moat,
hungry for me to be under control
to lose all sights my castle can hold,
waiting for war as it wades in the moat...

Early days for me

So stuck in my world I never leave here,
unless an other worlder asks me to,

needing me for things I turn minute --
I don't feel safe, a knife in my shoe -
something else close, a short body fifth,
inside is eight plus one that's nine -
times two,
now you have eighteen for goof troops......

Early in the day, right before dawn,
I crack a dark smile in my brain on...
in my world I don't folklore,
eating both sides, which
favors omnivores.

In apartheids
now a carnivore,
chewing on your bones 'til there is no more -
there is no more, there is no more!

Feelings are null if you enter my world,
hearts are used for makin' blood twirl,
keeping me alive, allowing me to twirl aloof!

Approaching midday, I raven to a small tree

then flip to a black owl with arched eyebrows,
prowling by eye from the air to the ground,
many souls came from Earth's lost ground,
looking to gain in my earthmound.

Its Dark out here

Accessible for the deepest of black,
the deepest of those who creep intact.
Hiding from corners between the cracks,
off to a land darker than your back.

Out in search for the brightness of dark
are pitch black men not afraid of the dark
in some dark world --- fresh dark winds,
eating the plants throughout the land.

This can be a place for some brave old men,
searching for peace lit worlds can't give.
A haven for women who want to build,
digging by hand for roots within -
old dark roots before they lived.

Grow Up

I saw it in a book,
to let them rise in sports or
let them make us laugh,
never nothing else.

A rally cry

Death to whom takes my hand for weak --
I was a sap who would always help out,
none helps me so I'm gritting my teeth,
drawing an end to my life on the couch.
I am of gold you won't find at church,
rather be cordial and share if I hold -
sharing brings danger,
with I don't flirt- like walking barefoot
through the deepest of snow.

Death to whom takes my hand for weak --
shortness of time won't allow me to act
as stupid consumers who follow the sheep,
I move with a big brain in my back pack --
to ready myself for the war within me ---
if we don't rap there is no pact.

Death to whom takes my hand for weak ---
at my wits end, done with the struggle.

Death to whom takes my hand for weak ---
don't you be caught in my streets...

Death to whom takes my hand for weak.

Another poem before bed
26 July 2015, 11:23 prime
(en la Floríd)

One against me can't see straight ahead -
I think as a maze so I fight with myself,
some use guns, scared of the pain -

I fight with my brain,
creating crop circles while finding
my way to Niccolas death ray, blatant no shame.
If they hate me, I might just sing ---:

*happy deathday, time to die
plain!*

Joking I do but playing I don't,
those who want will get their want,

splitting by three as a warning to don't -
the purest of me will secret to the bone,
hollow the waste and drink all the marrow ---
the worst of the worse, like trapped in snow
with super market money but no shovel,
you have been added to whom I don't know.

Early days for me, 2
27 July 2015   9:42 ante

A meeting with Maurice went well not swell, he said I resemble the red hells bells. Laughter we shared, deep inside his glare the glowing of caring was no longer there. What happened to him? Looks good and trimmed, something occurred and made him turn grim. He wished me peace, I nodded my head; to lose my doctor is something I dread; back to the world that houses my bed. What happened to him? Did he become me? Did I become him?

This can't be real!

(en La Florid)

Plural reception

If you're able to obtain anything
you're doing great!
Fuck other people, fuck what they think -

that 85' Chevy or
81' Ford ---
older model house with creaking floorboards,
pat your own back with a smile,
it's yours.

An old ten speed you had in 93',
still in good shape can handle the street
from A to B even well past C.
The job - the grocery – home - repeat.

If you're able to obtain anything
you're doing great,
life is a bar it's so easy to faint...
keep up with the who? Ain't my last name!
I'm at the yard sale lookin' through used things
and when I walk away I still feel great,
can go to the mall or shop Ebay,
fruits of my labor do not catch waste ---
happy I am to obtain anything.

The bright of Dark

all have choice all don't have voice,
all have hearts all don't have joice.
patterns are woven for regular men,
not many veer, most glue to it
permanently, permanent stupid.

painful to know then more so to see
the kinds of the breeds that litter the streets,
mimicking something they ate off tv ---
that icebox is lacking some eats,
off to the gym for that partial routine -
doing their best to undress critiques but
no one cares so fuck the referee,
and the referita......she cares neither...

this poem was written to
round the applause of
those with nothing in their jaws.

I'll get you

You know you have it coming,
so sleep, just sleep.
Any day I'll catch you,
til' just weep.

You know you have it coming,
so sleep, just sleep.
Once I make strike, I'll laugh you'll weep.
Ask yourself a question...

"why'd I play with him?"

Yes you've made an error, don't talk,
just think.
Spray you down with mine, open wide
don't blink.
Your pathway is brittle, one slip,
it breaks.

You know you have it coming,
so sleep, just sleep.

Mind games as I age

An outside glance,
a shirt
a pants,
shoes on the floor,
ass on the seat.
Who is this guy?
Yep,
that's me!

Eyes are shut with in depth peace,
furthering this --- I'm in a dream:

Poisons battle in my stomach,
drains to my legs then
under my feet,
menacing thoughts are following me.
Amity ghosts are following me,
wallowing false intrinsically.

Lingering souls in all black kilns are
trailing my path like spring break kids.

*"Come with us, come with us,
we bring a higher tier...
all your wants we have surplus,
come with us, we want you here!"*

The voices drift as billboard scripts
that surely cause good souls to flip.

"Come with us, we want you here!"

Gregory chants are all I hear,
I wake to feel my hair
decrease in length, then despair?
Wallowing ghosts have burned me well,
off I run away from hell -
so I thought?
I hear hells bells...
next are cries of clientele,
where am I to hear its bells?

Evenly odd, why burn my hair
and nothing else?
A thieving dream?
Even in peace they bother me...

Poetic wordplay

Where did midday go?
Lost between day and night,
not within range
like a ten hour flight -
shot like a gun that gauges by twelve
two-hundred miles away
is where the slug fell
as a time change
from east due west,
between the day break
and when the day fell!

Starting at one and lasting 'til eight -
prime meridian defines midday,
makes a whole third of one full day,
those of which are gauged by eights,
in the same sense
appearing everyday.

Circle of sand, quick

Draggin' you in, hands on both ears;
listen to me! So much will be said so
listen to me before I am dead!

Walking down the street I saw quick sand
in bi-pedal fad no mom no dad.
How can this be? Quick sand can stand?
Wearing a plant as the choice of my face
I laughed to see if the sand had shape,
had any hair or a womanly face -
all to be said is that sand was a blank.

Listen to me!
So much will be said so
listen to me before I am dead!

Crazy as daytime hours allow I
left my stupor, chased quick sand down.
For some strange reason no one was out,
my world is just me it all evens out.
If sealed tight as a young girls heart -
how did quick sand intrude my streets?
Being the me I know how to be,
Macheté connected at quik sands' knee.

Here is where things elevate to insane,

I open-hand smacked quik sand in the face
then quik sand flew all over the place,
sinking all scenery stuck in the way!
Someone give my small world a big shake,
change this draft to a small piece of cake -
clean through the wind is my timely escape
to the same place where planets are made.

Listen to me!
So much will be said so
listen to me before I am dead!

In my next draft, I know to watch out
for wild sand men followed by a strawman,
luring good hands into devilish gloves
which seem handmade by the worthiest scrubs.
Fracturing lives for a chance to repeat
the sandman trick planted under your feet.

Listen to me! So much will be said so
listen to me before I am dead!

Words from my pineal

Eyes allow the inside to see outside,
or allow the outside to see inside.
Seeing with ease the depths of skies,
viewing the life you feel inside,

waging wars by eye contact,
shakras beat when eyes blink back.

Look in my eyes - my heart beats back,
deep into my heart you can see my eyes.

Hair on my skin can listen and talk,
vibrantly hooked to the shakra stalk.
Searching the streets but not for talk,
sifting through death to find its pulse...

Eyes allow the inside to see inside,
those who know feel eyes don't lie -
eyes show hate on smiling faces...
look inside, see organs crying -
painting a still of your insides...
from the years of hurting self -
and from that can't see much else.

Eyes don't lie ---
ask anybody!

If it runs back,
tell everybody!
The gate to your soul,
life of your party.

Cemetary at dark

Oops, excuse me -
no mean to step on you,
I'm looking for a certain grave
maybe even two.
Here's my grandma! I view you in the dark -
darkness in my face, greatness in my heart.

Souls around me feel like humidity,
thick are the grips of death upon me -
dark is the face of this old cemetery.

From a latitude, graves are old bones
sprawled like grains of gloomy solitude --
maybe even domino's that don't fall.
From a longitude,
a black cape lays -
on top are white teeth
graciously spaced,
grass in between is a natural brace.

Back to a cypher -
deep in black I coin a catch phrase
that I speak to outerspace...
"peace to my grandma
and all others who layeth!"

Grave after grave, somber stories penetrate
deep caverns in my chest,
I should hallucinate!
The darker the night the more I feel safe.
Goblins and ghouls, and the Slenderman
will scare me straight -
wait up,
I just lied.
I don't play games with ghosts I tame lion.
Viewing the graves through funneled eyesight
- clinching my hands speaking to a dark night.

Macheta

Macheta wears a red dress
thin with the trim correct,
direct is her tongue in any dialect.

Speaking in terms harsher than kings can,
wielding one hand - Macheta owns land -
ruling as a woman rarely using two hands
to fight off trash, less dirt and more grass.

Grimly sincere, will share her yield though
coldly premier, no trace of a guild.
Balancing nature while battling evil,
handing out hands of love to her people.

Family is first, Macheta guards turf -
solidifies soils where most sink first.

Where art thou?

Where art thou dark night?
Within you I dress swell.
My ledger of life
is enhanced as I dance
in pure dark light,
healing in the night.
Feeding from foods that others fright,
stationing plants in no mans' land -
where people catch mud,
are stuck in a can
like college students
who crash in a cabin -
along came death
none knows what happened.

Don't play games

Through an open window flies an unwelcomed bird, gripped by its beak is what looks like a scroll. Its feathers are wilted from whatever battle; it claims a spot on the floor by the door --- one can see blood drenched on its worn talons. Those in the room shuffle thoughts they have of any brave act --- any quick escape route, pondering why a bird flew into the house. Filthy in color, it looks a yellow brown, the sight of this bird will make a cat growl – has the eyes of clouds, sight is surround. Feasting its sight on the six sold souls, this old bird is looking for its out --- stuck in its mouth is a map of the grounds, noting every safehouse hid from the town. These six souls are childhood friends --- none of them thought of hell as this. All six souls are forced to read the scroll, following orders of losing their soul.

Fetch

"Where are you going?" Asked Truth as her uncle put his left shoe on while unevenly looking for the right.

"I'm going to the library real quick while I still can…I'm bored plus tv is stupid," replied Uncle Intent.

"While you still can, what does that mean, the libwawy is still there right?" Asked Truth.

"Be quiet, you weren't supposed to catch what I said…powderkeg head girl," joked Uncle Intent.

"I wanna go!" Truth exclaimed as always, seemingly ignoring her Uncles' lame talk.

"Alright well come on, let's go brush our teeth, then find ya' shoes and go tell ya' daddy we 'bout ta leave, 'lil blockhead girl."

"Alright uncle," went Truth, playfully slapping him on his back.

As Uncle Intent and Truth started toward the bathroom, a coin drop filled the air. "Uncllllllle, your phone," cartooned Truth, as she reached for her pink bubblegum toothbrush. Uncle Intent paid it no attention and advanced to the cabinet to get his raggedy toothbrush and paste then began to brush his teeth alongside of his niece.

"All done!" Elated Truth, now rinsing with water.

"Same here," stated Uncle Intent as he opened his mouthwash, always mimicking the good habits of his niece despite the twenty-seven-year age gap. "Go tell ya' Daddy we gone and get my keys off the table…" he murpled to Truth, in between gargles.

"Alright Uncle…heyyy, are you going to get that text?"

"Text? How you know I got a text?"

"Because I know everything," assured Truth.

"At four years old, you probably do, but anyways… go t-"

"-- I'm going to tell daddy I'm leavin'," Interjected Truth.

"Children, I swear," went Uncle Intent to himself.

Truth skipped out of the bathroom then ran to the back of the house and, while holding the rail, walked carefully down the wooden steps that led to the basement where her father was washing clothes.

"Daddyyy," babied truth, calling out to her father Grinold.

"What lil' girl," said Grinold with a joker face grin.

"Me and Uncle are going to the libwawy."
"What?"
"I said Uncle and me are going to the libwawy."
"The what? Oh…the library. So, you just goin'… just like that though? What happened to actually *asking me* if you could go?"
"Uncle said to *tell* you."
"Ya' uncle is *lost*, you know that and you know to ask; so next time ask, alright? Now gimmee a hug, you look like a bug."
"Daddyyy, that's craaazy," replied Truth while hugging her father as they laughed together.
"See you later baby, be gooood," Grinold wished to his daughter. While he and Truth were talking, Uncle Intent grabbed his phone from the table in the breakfast nook, unlocked it and began reading the text that Truth was talking about. It was from Easul, his old college buddy of the same age…

"Man hurry up, we close shortly
 and somebody might notice they gon'."
[4:37 prime]

Uncle Intent thought to himself that he had better hurry the hell up and leave before he misses out on a good opportunity. As he wound down his thoughts, Truth made her way up the steps and to her uncles' side. "Alright Uncle, I'm ready," said Truth, smiling at her Uncle.

"Good, vamos joven," said Uncle Intent, no pun intended.

"Stop with that spanish Uncle…oops, I meant to say Watin, right?"

"Latin, right. Good job! Now *vamos* joven, I think I'm late," groaned Uncle Intent, placing his hand on Truths' head as they walked through the almost Victorian styled house, out through the front door then down the steps to his black Cadillac Deville. He humanely secured Truth in her carseat, opened the drivers' door, started the car then switched gears as fast as he could. It was Indian Summer out in Ami Nation, so the weather was warm, photogenic and described as *ideal*. Sky blue paint and large bright clouds of history filled the early September day. As he and Truth maneuvered through the so called suburban area, and all its children, to Empiez Boulevard, two loud coin drop notifications sounded out almost simultaneously throughout the serene environment inside of the Deville. Uncle Intent pulled over slowly, ensuring Truth wasn't inconvenienced by a sudden stop. There was basically no traffic on the calm un-named streets of the suburbs, so he was able to quickly read the text. It was sent with high alert…

Easul:
"...Did you get the last text son?
 You gotta' hurry up..."
[4.43 prime]

Me:
"...Yea, my bad you know me.
I'm on the way now."
[4:44 prime]

Uncle Intent threw his car into drive and got back on the street. He knew he had to hurry up and being about two miles from the Crimson Expressway he could catch up on lost time. The Materplex Library was about three miles off the Gateway Avenue exit, but the exit is about fifteen miles down the expressway; a possible twenty-minute drive. Consisting of three towering stories of indispensable information, the Materplex is the most saturated library in Ami Nation; it looks of antiquity in its one-hundred and seventy-five-year architecture, but it has modern sidewalks due to the original sidewalk being broken apart during a family war for control of the libraries resources back in the year 1840. Apparently, not only the gringo had interests in the Materplex. There are also three statue lionesses evenly situated on its roof-ledge where one might expect to see gargoyles. As the Deville neared the Pixie on-ramp, here goes Truth...

"Uncle, are you about to go fast?" She asked.

"Yea I am …"

"I like fast, it's like fwiying right?" Inquired Truth. She sometimes pronounces the letter "l"or "r" like one would pronounce the letter "w", because she's goofy and of course learning from adult talk as she's an only child; a brat if you will. She never falls short of responses.

"Yea I guess you're flying now, but don't try to unlock your seatbelt, if you do I'll kick you in your back," joked Uncle Intent while laughing aloud. Merging into saturday traffic on the Crimson Expressway was a breeze compared to workweek traffic, plus; not many highway men would be out – and if they were, he could tell. He powered through medium traffic into the fast lane and began to speed a little, to about eighty miles per hour. The speed limit on the Crimson was seventy miles per hour. Two more coin-drop notifications roared through the speakers, but Uncle Intent was busy watching traffic and never did dare to text and drive. Truth was stuck looking at cars whiz by and made no mention of the coins. Both were essentially occupied and didn't even comment.

Feeling pressed for time, Uncle Intent pushed his Deville to about eighty-five miles per hour in the fast lane. He knew who the text was probably from and he knew that he had all day to get to the library; but now, he may miss out on a good opportunity on something he's been wanting for years; sad. Close to five minutes have passed since that last text from Easul and Uncle Intent was still rolling down the Crimson. "You alright back there limelight?" Silence filled the car. "Aye," he started… "are you…" He quit his speech as he looked in the rearview and saw Truth was well past fast asleep. He giggled to himself and kept in the fast lane. As he neared the Gateway Avenue exit, his heartbeat began to increase as if it was speaking "opportunity!" It was now every bit of 4: 56 prime and the black Deville digressed down the exit ramp onto Gateway Avenue. The Materplex Library was about three minutes away and Uncle Intent was nearing his destination. He blew through a yellow light but stayed within the thirty-five miles per hour speed limit on the avenue. As he saw the library come into view, two more text notifications sounded off and he knew they had to be from Easul. The time was now every bit of 4:59 prime, and the black Deville finally pulled into the gravel of the Materplex to see two men carrying a long black couch out of the front door. *"Dam, they really closing this place huh? It's been here for decades and I ain't been here in years,"* Uncle Intent thought to himself. "C'mon Truth, we here…", but of course no response from

Truth as she was slumbering hard. He got out of the car, opened Truth's door rather slowly, picked her up, placed her over his shoulder then started toward the front door of the library. Rich assortments of beautiful flowers, healthy palm trees, big elephant ears, random bushes, tall trees and old brick engulfed the strong aesthetics of the Materplex. The gravel lot was about a twenty second walk to the library door, and as Uncle Intent neared the steps he could see his old friend Easul looking right at him, smiling from ear to ear. Right before he and Truth made it to the last step before the door, Easul placed a finger on his lips for them to be quiet and began whispering as he held the front door open for the duo.

"Nigga you barely made it," Easul whispered, while smiling and shaking' hands with his old friend. "You know they burned Alexandria, so c'mon we ain't got all day -- follow me, I got ya' stuff downstairs," he continued. Uncle Intent followed Easul around the empty front desk area to some back offices that eventually led to a staircase down to the basement or lower level. By this time, Truth was snoring, still in her Uncle's arms. About fifteen wooden steps led to the basement, and the staircase, though old, seemed to be well kept. There was a light at the bottom of the steps and Easul was already close, as if he jumped. Uncle

Intent took about five steps before he could sense the typical thick air of an older buildings' lower levels. If the air was too thick for his niece to breathe, he would have to wait in the well while Easul went wherever he was going. Luckily, as he stepped, he could hear ceiling fans whirling and noticed very faint light emitting from the retired fluorescents. By the time Uncle Intent made it to the basement, Truth had awakened, widely.

"Where we at bruh?" Truth asked as if she knew to keep a low voice. "Are we in the libwawy?"

Uncle Intent laughed a little before responding. "Yea," he whispered. "Talk in your little voice until we leave, alright?"

"Alright," whispered Truth, placing her hands over her mouth. Out of nowhere, they heard a faint knocking sound, and noticed an open closet door in a dimly lit hallway if one went right once they walked down the steps. Easul was the source of the faint knocking. He went into a closet and tapped twice on the wall to open something; seemingly like a trap door, only it was located on the wall. Out he pulled a large, rather new looking black gym bag.

"Here you go man," said Easul, handing over the bag to Uncle Intent. "To think, they were gonna' throw these books away. Shit, they wasn't even lettin' mufukas check em' out. It's a few older Blacks' in here, real old dictionaries, Webster's, books of old ass maps, all this shit is old," babbled Easul in excitement.

"Hell na', I see you still the same with the hiding places. Thanks for all this. Now I can show what I mean rather than say it. Plus, my history teacher has failed my last two papers for no reason. I tell her I'm good at history and she for real laughs, and on top of all that she's darker than me; straight hateful. I ain't gon' fail this third paper, and she gon' re-grade those other papers," declared Uncle Intent.

"Yo' ass don't respond to texts and all slow as hell, you almost missed out. This library closed for good today at five o'clock, it's now like five-ten; you lucky you in the building, period," said Easul.

"Uncle is always slow," added Truth and of course Uncle Intent chuckled, Easul laughed too.

"So look, Ms. Santos, the owner of Materplex Incorporated, is upstairs right now; not on the first but on the second floor. Now listen; yea her surname is Santos, but her skin is darker than mine yo'. Now, her assistant Ms. Bernstein is here also and she's straight up European; neither of them are playin' with niggas. If they catch me doing this we all through, done, *muerto*! She's very cordial and all but we gotta' be quiet the whole time we here," babbled Easul. "They gon' be here til' about six-thirty, they--." Before he could continue, Easul was interrupted by the booming voice of Ms. Santos.

"Easuuuuulll……where are you honey? Me and Lisa need coffee please….…Are you there, or did you go to help he moving guys eh? You're always helping someone, but we need coffeee," she comically pleaded.

Though she was up maybe two levels, her voice was faintly yet easily heard from where the group was in the basement; possibly due to the old ass ventilation systems of the Materplex. Uncle Intent and Easul were nervous as hell now, Truth was looking around in awe. "Is that Ms. Santos?" She whispered.

"Yea," went Easul, pulling his cellphone from his pocket. "It's easy to hear her from the second floor because the library has an open layout, but you couldn't tell from where yaw came in; but follow me, I got an idea. She won't come down this far." In tandem they quickly crept to another set of stairs at what seemed like the end of the hallway. There was no telling if Ms. Santos was going to start looking for him or stay busy in her books. "I'ma text her and tell her I'm in the bathroom," said Easul. "That'll surely buy us some time."

"What about us?" Questioned Truth in her little voice. Even in the odd moments, she's right on time.

"Don't worry Ms. Truth," replied Easul with a smile. "I'll show you how to get outta' here." He then began to text Ms. Santos.

> Easul:
> "Hey, just letting you know I went to the bathroom. It'll be a while. LOL"
> [5:13 prime]

"Alright, let's see what she says." Before his phone screen could even dim, Ms. Santos replied...probably by voice text.

Ms. Santos:
"Mijo, spare the details. I was just looking for you, we need some coffee while we're doing these books. Eh, It's alright, I'll have Malay make it."
[5:15 prime]

Easul laughed aloud at the text. Malay, from Asia, was Ms. Santos' nineteen-year-old understudy with a brown nose, and those type of people can be very nerve-wrecking which is why Ms. Santos always called on Easul for everything. Malay is cool and all, but she's too gitty; way too much so.

> Easul:
> "Sorry, lol...see you later
> ..."
>
> [5:16 prime]

"Aight yaw, that was easier than I thought. We good for now," continued Easul, seemingly excited. "These stairs will lead us to an old office area that no one uses, but I'ma still check to make sure she's not lingerin' around anywhere."

"Yea I bet you will genius," stated Uncle Intent. "That ladies' voice scared me to death, just to even hear it. It's so quiet down here...then bam! The voice of Ms. Santos. Me and Truth feel crazy right now."

"Yea, real cwazy dude," Truths little voice sparked. The guys tried hard not to laugh at Truth, but they couldn't help it and all three of them shared a low toned giggle. Knowing now it was no telling when Ms. Santos would pop back up because understudies don't make good coffee, they just don't, Easul motioned to be followed and quickly disappeared around a sharp corner behind the stairwell. Once Uncle Intent and Truth caught on to Easul, he was at the top of another short stairwell, standing under a dim exit sign.

"Dam, do you do this often?" Whispered Uncle Intent, holding Truth tight as they scaled the short case.

"Na' never I just know this place, you know I been here like three years. I would be dumb not to know the ins and outs son. See look, there's the parking lot right there, and you came in the library wayyy back that way," went Easul. Sure enough, the parking lot was in close view and Uncle Intent could see his empty Cadillac.

"That would be *allí* and *allá*," goofied Uncle Intent.

"What?" Asked Easul.

"*Allí* means there, and *allá* means over there. I'm teachin' myself spanish."

"You do that," said Easul, pointing toward the parking lot.

"Aye, what happened to those moving guys; the ones that me and Truth saw as we pulled in here?" Asked Uncle Intent.

"Yo,' good question!" Exclaimed Easul, lightly. "Aye, these top CEO people play no games about throwing stuff away. You know how couches eat people change or whatever fall outta' they pocket? Well, instead of having me or someone else check the couches for lost itemry, they have a special clean up team to do it."

"Whaaa?! That's crazy as hell. What they doin?"

"See my point…be lucky you got them books nigga. That was the only couch left in here that only select people sat on while in the conference rooms. Ain't no other couches so they ain't coming back. Now let's make sure you make it outta' here unnoticed so I can remain un-scaved," replied Easul. As they scoured the property from the view of the exit door, they could see nothing but the same four sedans that marked the presence of the four employees inside of the Materplex: *Easul, Ms. Santos, Mrs. Bernstein, and Malay.* The black deville was parked in a row by itself, behind the other cars. It made so much sense to just walk out through the exit door, but for some reason *nobody* budged.

"Easuuuuul!" Went the faint sound of Ms. Santos. "Where are you my dear?"

How they were able to hear her is beyond all of them; like she was involuntarily on the same path as them, a floor or so above, speaking directly down into a vent. Didn't Malay make that coffee…...? Still in the stairwell awaiting their next move, all three of the eager souls seemed to have lost blood; all had wide open eyes and mouths like a Halloween mask would have. The trailing voice of Ms. Santos caught them off-guard big time. *What do you think*? Easul quickly yanked his cellphone from his pocket and dialed Ms. Santos like he had her on speedial.

"Ola Easul!" She answered on a half-ring.

"Where are you sweety? That coffee Malay tried to make just failed. Can you please help me?"

"Yes mam, I can help you. Sorry I was just in the basement making sure that all windows where locked, ya' know; double checking things since we are finally closing this place."

"Very good mijo, I would not have thought about the windows right now. It's just time to move forward, for all of us. You remember the figures I showed you in that report, right? You saw it for yourself, not many people in this area truly read real books anymore, everything is online somehow — kindle or PDF format. Nobody wants a real book."

"Yea that's sad Ms. Santos, but when we get to the new area of town, we'll feel like nerds again."

"Jajaja," she laughed. "Alright honey, we are still upstairs with the blinds shut, waiting for that coffee. I'm so tired, if I look outside I'm going home mijo! Ay yi yi! When you are finished, please hurry because I have ordered pizza for all of us from Tres Amigos. It'll be here in about twenty minutes. You can't even get that pizza until after eight o'clock."

"Really? I love that pizza!"

"Yes really, and it's on the house. Yo conozco Macheté from way back, he has a real heart of gold, but watch out, he's dangerous."

"I kinda' heard that about him, he seem

cool tho'. Just a few more windows to check and I'll be right up," Easul finished.

"Alright honey, luego," said Ms. Santos, ending the call.

"We gon," inferred Uncle Intent. "It's gettin' wild in here and that lady's voice carries. Thanks again for these books man!"

"Aye no problem man," responded Easul as he and Uncle Intent shook hands, waving at Truth as she smiled and waved back. "Don't forget, we moving to a new location, I'll keep you posted. No tellin' what that library gon' have." Easul threw Uncle Intent the deuces, and without giving him a chance to respond he drifted back down the basement steps and disappeared into the darkness of the Materplex. Once out through the exit door, Truth and Uncle Intent hurriedly made their way through the vague parking lot to the awaiting Deville. The once sunny day about twenty minutes ago now seemed dismal and blank. Uncle Intent secured Truth in her carseat, prying her from his arms while remaining vigilant of the grounds around them. Not a single soul was in sight and the avenue was oddly quiet for a weekend. He quickly started his car, eased into gear and drove out of the parking lot onto Gateway, viewing the Materplex for the last time.

ii

The pathway of Macheté

Years of maltreatment before me is this,
decades of knowing laid in the cement
made it to light where the bright of it is,
now I can frolic in spite of the hyks -
helping only me, so I see well,
America was strong even when Ghana fell,
had the very name and the land wasn't plain -
fell into shame when the shady man came.

A story not told is of that who sold
me out to people who froze my soul.
Stole my story and made their gold,
wrote their story to stop my growth.

The marksmanship of a pen

Inert but ready, like cold war nukes
is a man who will go with or without you.
Scaling a mountain with only a tack,
angry at knives stuck in their backs,
knives in their thighs -- hurt in their eyes.
Made great attempts to mend the fell off,
since they didn't care, friendships are off.

A chance to be my friend? Bets are strictly off.
Not a random sniper who cannot calm pace,
a mad man thinks mad ways to evade
and to never be seen by typical fate ---
typical humans who live the slow way.
Nowhere can you look when a mad man plays

A slight breeze

A cold heart breathes just like a warm heart,
though on different sides of life's thermostat;
both pump blood to the same body parts,
watering yards of different cataracts -
fueling large tanks of different regard.
Cold hearts see what warm hearts deny,
looking the same by the
face on its card,
in the same cell, sleep on different sides.

A warm heart breathes just like a cold heart,
smiling at times where the cold heart's broke,
still in good soul if it catches a dart
from cold heart foes who let hate show.

None can bring chill to great warm hearts,
even in the snow warm hearts never slow.

The coldest of hearts will fail at the rail
of true warm hearts who melt each snow.

Where darkness fell

Upon me -
quickly,
swift as can be,
everything fell
and my poetry!
Heart turned flat -
blood went sub-
zero on the richter,
what do I do?
Fairytales end
when dreams come true -
does *when* come
when nightmares bloom?

Upon me,
quickly -
dark as it could be
a nightmare came
in a bright red dress
and swore she's never came!
Crazy as I am
I saw the bit apple,
still took the bait
like that foolish Adam -
my soul left Earth...
landed on Castor,

took a look at Pollux and
called his ass a bastard...
the solar system smiled
'cause a gemini is standing.

I'm getting tired

Much should be done to
correct my mistakes --
correcting my mistakes has
me dressed in all black:
on the frontline with a black hardhat,
looking for the traitors
who stabbed me in the back
and stripped my blood in one mean act!
Took my plasma and killed my cats,
killed my dogs -
that's all I had!
Made me cry like someone died,
in my dark nights -
no one dies!
Fuck outta' here where no one cries,
emotions don't live ---
they dry out like mankind did
coming to America!

Night fuel, brief

This garden of fruit
was here before the
sun was loose.
Seeds grew through
the night indeed and
bred a crop of en Sanguine
for the brights of dark to eat.

Colón would say

He didn't find us here
he saw us from shores...

...land with fruits and berries indeed,
not far from water, enclosed by trees.

Down he wrote with truthfulness:

"...Here they live with such delight,
froze I am at sights of them,
I can see they move with skill,
copper is the skin of them.

Looking around, I see great land,
not can I see one pale skin man -
that pale skin that we have there
is not right here, it seems so rare!

(*In conclusion...*)

This western land is far from plain,
they were here before I came..."

Purposeless Mf's

On the same sheet as fiat
is the same sheet of birth,
to that second father its
a seal that proves the sale,
reveals the awful curse
leading to unlawful girth -
slavery is here but its
hidden by the colors
of your phone cases and
of some mixed brothers,
and some mixed sisters you
can't find in a cupboard.

On the same sheet as fiat
is the same sheet of birth-
History repeats but
its founded in the dirt -
leading them in years but
they hit us where it hurts -
all across the world are
the feelings of the hurt -
many lost souls have
been blinded by the curse.

Hot media?
Molding people into slurps!

Dam tv
changing souls for the worse,
changing into devils
to ravage mother Earth...

The Game

They say Jesus wept -
again,
they say -
how could he weep much
if the letter called "J"
was not in use at
the time Jesus wept?

What is his real name?
Take a look back at
the time they say that
Jesus wept, no letter J
found in any alphabet,
what can I say?
Find who he was
before the letter J.

Questions, 2

If I draw my flag will it drip my blood?
Questions for the cell base of my audience.
If I start now will I finish my run
with two black guns, waiting for a pun?
Why wait for when the five has eight,
the khae has a hundred and
they day's gon' fade?

Questions for the cell base of my audience -
Is it obvious life is a cute bitch?
Leave me a comment for this argument:
Skinny jean pants and the odd tattoos
are less dangerous than a dude in a suit -
then again wait,
they can be the same.

Questions for the cell base of my audience,
leave me a comment for this argument:
people really voted for a black president
only just because - the color of his skin...

...My answer...
life is a lying bitch.

De la noche, a brief

Don't crucify me,
I wanted to be right,
lend helping hands to
minors in the fight,
was a good friend when
I knew it to be right.

Don't crucify me,
I grew into a man
with big wide eyes -
everybody knows me!
If or not they like
that means no such, who
the fuck knows you?
Let me make my point!

Don't crucify me,
I bit my tongue again -
to fix my broke tongue I
wear a Joker grin,
minus purple suits
I'm being gon' again
like a gon' good girl who
quit being good again.

Don't crucify me!

Fuck Friendz

I took a deep thought and made my mind,
those fake friends cannot be mine.
Never can be - never can be –
never can be
a friend to me.

"Forget who I am,
shave this fat until I'm thin,
wash my hair and scrub my skin -
help me rid of fleas and ticks
that wrongly won't let go of me
but truly have no love for me!"

I know their secrets - know their pain,
that means squat they let me hang,
let me hang, let me hang -
never will I friend again...

I'm not your friend

Far in my lair -
chiseling arms for me to fair,
locking my hair,
deep in the game where nobody cares,
loving myself,
atoms repaired -
why be good in life unfair -
race is a snare -
tears in a belt or
bugs in your hair- distracting affairs;
holes in your truth for national stance,
tears in your palms -
blood in your hands,
that's what it takes for any advance...
...careful in dance.

What time is it?

Ahora es mi tiempo,
Para creciendo la pais
donde
mi frutas crecen con no veneno
Necesito mas calor mi corazón frio,
Ahora es mi tiempo, antes soy viejo
¿Donde esta Macheta?
¡Ella mejor prisa!
Sacame a la tienda, comprame un desert eagle,
Ayudame a respirar, antes salgo mi vida…

Random Poetic Violence

I don't know if I care at all,
sometimes I dream of numerous scenes-
In most of them I seem to fall,
other times I'm very mean.
Falling means I lost a fight
or I quickly ran away,
means is when I came to you
then I shot you in the face,
broad day,
took a few notes then made my escape.
As sure as wind blows and fiat is printed,
I always take time to note how I feel.

Before or after

When will I live?
Hopefully before I die.
When will I smile?
Hopefully before I cry,
    or after,
to me sometimes it truly doesn't matter.
I brace myself to face the worse
then end it all in laughter.

Macheté wept

Can I walk away from the pain I feel?
 What was one could be again.
Can I run away when it's on my heel?
 From my soul I lose an inch.
Do I find a way to become free will?
 From my heart I lose a pin.
Do I look around when it can't be real?
 In my eyes I gain a grip.
Will I make it far with an old windmill?
 In my legs I heal my chins.
Is it right for me if I take then give?
 In my hands I hold a deal.
Is a better life on its way up hill?
 From a far I hear its cheer.
Shall I stay away if it can't be real?
 From the midst a cloud appears.
Shall I call it quits if I get mad still?
 What was once could be again.

From a certain standpoint

Can self be lost behind the scenes?
It once was here but now a dream,
fell hard and then went up the street
running themselves into debris,

Self was lost behind the scenes
it was not allowed to breathe,
so itself it could not be.
Forced in clothes to play a scene,
but those clothes will never leave,
self was lost behind the scenes.

Fuego

I write I read I think I may
go build a house of thick mache
in the woods all by myself
I see me as someone else
not that I have withered stealth
but I need to better self
take sometime to ease myself
can't afford to lose myself
I must learn to heal myself.

Drop you off in Iceland

If you not american but hate to be yourself, just go back to where you came from because we don't need you nor your sad song, your family nor your tag along. Take what you have and fly back to Africa, find where you claim to be stolen from and set post with the locals, before sunset your feet will be smokin', legs will be hurtin', skin will be burnin', so called homeland gave you a scolding. What you will eat, you cannot pronounce it, that you arrived, no one will announce it. You at home though? Even they know that what doesn't look like can't be it, you have no place so you can't be them. Being as it may, go to iceland and you will see that it's green and greenland is ice- how can that be right? One more thing, I'm american, american again- simple and plain, where I attach is not for debate.

Canister of air

Right back at you do I stare straight through,
give me what you have or I'll run full speed
at your forhead with a bubblegum chew
you might know them but you don't know me.
For the greater good never will be you-
You have two eyes but you don't have these,
what you lay claim to came from a group,
everything I found out came through me.

Enough said.

The contagion

Make your own bed and you lay in it too
people act funny and know what they do
caught you at first when you tried to help out
thought I was stupid because of my smile
hiding from me like I would not find out
knew of your danger because of my mouth
shut ya' ass down by the words that came out
now you are different I'm hearing you pout
not did you think that I would figure out.

Being me myself

A feature of those who oppose
are the same
as those who don't,
pick em' straight apart and
release the demon that leads them on,
not to save them but to
save the rest of me that's
embedded in my lawn.

Before a napmare

If at all I did this often ---

nap away a day or live half awake,
slumber in my speech, going free fall
down an unknown street, stuffing my cake
all in my face before I'm called -
caught in awe of meaningless fate,
meaningless gifts of meaningless cause.
Pulling me over, it's easy to see
my plates are valid; don't kick me in the balls
or take my legs so I can't go home.

Cranberries for everyone!

Come and grab some of this -
get a fair share
before this one-time tide gets low -
drying to dirt never to show.

If you missed on your fare share -
obtained some fruit from somewhere else,
pure cranberries you do not have!

A Christmas carol!!!

I have blank checks for a very low price,
paying the orders of typical vice -
viewing the ledger without blinking twice,
shuffling names one cannot recite
without the skills of a thief in the night
dope on the science of sighting the bright,
privy to paths one can travel at night
and meeting the king where no one can see,
nothing can hear but the ears of the trees,
the ears of the grass the ears of the seeds.

I have blank checks for a very low price -
paying the orders of typical vice,
salting the streets with the heaviest ice,
melting the price that was put on my life.
Taking the rifle and checking it twice,
it better be loaded - better shoot right!
Thinking about who's been naughty not nice,
changing the weather to ruin my life.
Before it was salted I chewed the streets,
tasted the poison before it was ripe.

I have blank checks for a very low price -
paying the orders of typical vice,
softening stools of the lingering might,
breaking them down to a liquid of hype,

hearing them beg from the laxative fright,
finally caught is the muddiest sight,
mud in their pants as they cry through the night -
knowing the end of the scam is in sight.

I have blank checks for a very low price,
paying the orders of typical vice.

Recruiting, a De la noche sonnet

Tonight is the night to fill up the pots,
souls we have stolen by napping adults
straight from their bed of their humble abodes,
sealing their mouths with the dirtiest socks,
into the bus where their bodies are stored
no window posted they cannot see out,
they know it's the time and so they bow down.

"Who are you people, where are we going?

They cry out in fear and all have been tied
together in chains, they cannot escape
random collection the easiest way;
noting on people and learning their lives.
Tonight is the night to fill up the pots -
storing the people away from the fox.

Archery

On a bent knee I take my seat,
out of range is where I'll be -
dodging scums of hateful creed,
mad at me for what I am
is what they can't nor ever be.
Blasphemy as they call him,
warning shots will cause a limp -
stubborn folks still sing their hymns
even if their master's dead,
stubborn folks still kiss his head.

' De Facto '

                        I thought she was right,

looked left -

                                she was gone!

...Just am

Understand that -
I'm under your bed,
understand that
I'm in your closet.
Understand this -
not in your shoes
I took the shoe laces --
whatchu' gon' do?

To the Elders

Without seeing trees,
without seeing sun,
I know I'd fail,
I know I would.

Without feeling woman -
around too many men -
I know I'd fail,
I swear I would.

Without mother nature
I am not father nature -
I know I'm not,
there is no way.

Inertia

The balance of my shapes
and sizes infiltrate the
guises in the
hearts of mizers...

give it up!!!

Nothing but wordplay, that's all

It's three on the square,
one on the bilgrin -
three on the bilgrin and
one on the square,
one on the bilgrin
that houses the square -
three in the square that
houses the bilgrin,
all on the land
that's built for the bilgrin -
none on the land
that's built for the Pilgrim.

A question for...who?

Where are the problem solvers,
nearing alcoholic?
Have you seen our world?
It's coming out the closet,
hidden worldly truths
are pounding on your door -
put your phone down --
go see what's in store!

*"A great dissolution 'til
there is no more!"*

The great atom bomb has
awaken from its snore.
A nuketown map has
arisen to its shores,
none can dodge the heat,
the richest nor the poor.

Hello; Biatch

A full circle ride from here to there
not there to here,
I've always been here!
History tells the quietest tale of
wars and pacts, and dangerous spell -
watch for the package you get in the mail,
watch for the people that look for the sale;
the preacher at post,
the choir of ghosts;
practice a way to not fall in the moat,
fall down the hill or
fall down the slope.
Do what you can to escape the remote.

!!!Free Lunch!!!

As I step outside on a calm summer night;
nothing is stirring, not even my delight -
looking at the sky all I see are my eyes,
in between planets I can see my Gemini,
boiling human stew and the aliens aside -
baking body cakes while they eat brain pie,
call it brain food as they chatter and assume,
chatter and assume, chatter and assume
that I need their chatter for what I do,
haven't they heard that one who assumes
is dead as a garden that does not bloom
in tropical weather, dead as a shoe?

Watch what you eat in that free lunch stew.

Life has no script

Can you see what you have?
Much is in store if
the street mixes with the heat
into an omnivore,
vegetables talk as they
grow from the stalk,
meat cries hell as
it's cut from the hog.
See what I mean?
I rather eat a leaf or
a bundle of leaves rather
than dead meat
that's not cooked right, leaving
blood in my teeth.

"The Heat, the heat"

So called blacks don't speak about much,
how to be the same is what they discuss.
Claiming free reign on the back of the bus,
not man enough to escape from the bus.

!Don't do it, Macheté!

Fluently;
not afraid of those
in the trickery -
from the first homeland,
healthy without tanning,
I am not your friend
don't argue with me,
where I play in dark you
can't frolic with me,
throw your towel in,
seeing much terrain, nearing
midlife's dream,
stop following me -
I do not have a team,
everybody's dead and
I only care for me
and the blood I share
with the ancient in my tree.

Fluently;
not afraid of those
in the trickery.

The Codex

Before nightfall came truth in the fog;
thick summer heat brought day walk crawl,
just after dusk came mail in the cusp
of two black ducks looking for gold tusks -
cutting through fog just to reach great laws
left on walls the size of a mall next
to another mall built for a greater cause;
freeing the souls that were caught in a thaw
free trapped souls so engulfed by a boat
of cold gringos with disease for the Earth,
curse for the ones drinking sunlight first --
before nightfall came a thief for the purse.

The missings

I lost what I had and it made me mad,
took a back seat on my own dam map.

Full as it is life didn't make sense,
couldn't make out the sounds on the
lips of my souls' inner grip
shaped like a space ship,
needing a charge of its energy grid -

I lost what I had and it made me mad,
lost all I had and it made me sad,
much of me was lost for I had so much,
dull life forms went gold from my touch -
but...
I fell apart from the touch,
touch after touch I lost so much;
gold I was giving
but ashes I received,
took a base metal from my normal energy,
left me to a putty and colic as I breathe.

Approximately

Take a brick hard dick
and a brick hard dick;
What do you get?
Interesting shit.

With no offense
don't forget women.

Astral Plane

Once I fly away
I may not come back...

I let my locks hang
so I don't wear caps.

In a copper state
I cover big maps.

My Grandma said
as the wise turn weak
the asses flatten
out of the seat.

I'm using granny's sense
to make a better me,

Disrespect granny and
I'll put you in a tree,
play target practice
with your two front teeth.

I'm using granny's sense
to make a better me

in my inner-self

I don't watch T.V.

Once I learn how
you will not see me,

fruit I can grow
in my own galaxy.

The Heat, again

Who I must be cannot be you,
this you claim I see right through.
One dark night at you came two
real men with metal at you,
eight in the clip and one in the groove,
give me the screws you put in the stew -
breaking my teeth apart as I chew,
bleeding my gums as life falls through -
pay what you owe for monies are due,
heats of the hurt are pointed at you.

Vitality Molecules

So many times I look to the sky,
why do I feel and why do I cry?
Hard as I am, I'm soft at the same,
time after time I'm dark while awake -
raining in thought I'm stuck when I think -
looking for fiat is giving me rage -
give me a breath or give me a death -
watching the ground for cracks as I step,
who is the crook who taketh my breath
and taketh my life away from myself...?

They 'tryna give me the black plague man!

With no respect to color - they feed me illnesses, wishing for a shedding at my world class skin. Poisoning my heart by way of throwing darts athot air balloons in my sky since my start - lyin' to my face 'bout the way they give cards, livin' as a john praying to a pale god - never are they sorry for they don't' have hearts, can't grow fruit but the cancer they enlarge, feathers from their birds fall in my front yard -screams from the youth cast spells from the yard, onto the porch - through the front door - now the whole house is suffering sores.

Why won't they?

The hearts of guys who lost their eyes
to soft asides that whisper high-
give me that and you get this,
this is yours but you lost that.
Once you see I know you'll cry,
choose to fall or choose to rise.
In the field of stolen eyes,
soul is gone until you die.

The hearts of guys who lost their eyes
to soft asides that whisper high-

A statement

I could care *less* what niggas think -
I know who I am;
that's all that it takes.

A different start, but worthy... LOL

Cataracts
for my cataracts
on top of cataracts -
give me all the smokies,
the rest is irrelevant.
Lively in the pines
with the rosiest of elegance -
I can see the light;
darkest of the might -
keeping all the greetings
that see me through the fog,
careful in this no wash cloth free for all.

Announcement 1

I feel much hate from the weaker brigade,
niggas show place takin' orders from the base;
never can they know -
never can they throw a
first aid kit on a live boomerang.

Fuck you niggas -
wannabees and the like,
Fuck you niggas -
bitch I said the shit twice!

I gave em' a chance but
niggas tried to cutt my hand -
causing me to walk soft on my own land?

In my high mind, straight from the above,
I take a deep breath to alleviate scum.

Who

   Was

         I

             talking to?

The 5:30 bus blew past Yeta Yonas even though she waved for it to stop, running frantically. "Fuck!" She exclaimed. "I'm always late." It was rather hard for the bus driver to see Yeta in the dusk if she wasn't at least somewhat visible. There was much underbrush and spanish moss hanging from the live oak trees that swamped the area before the walkway to the bus stop began; she was nowhere near the drivers' sight.

Intending to arrive at work early, she would have to wait to catch the 5:50 bus to be there well before 6:30 ante-meridian. It was early in the day and already hot in La Floríd. Yeta wiped her brow with a pocket napkin and threw it away in the nearby trashcan. Placing both hands on her face, she massaged her brain a little. "Man, I guess I really do need to start driving," she thought aloud. "I can't keep being late for work." It was close to about a twenty-five-minute ride in town- well, to Meri Gardens, the area of town where she worked- and Yeta always caught the city/county bus to save money, so she thought. Narrowing down her thoughts, she started walking toward the actual bus stop and *that's* when she saw him, a man; posted in a corner of the stop shelter. There was never anyone out nor on the bus stop when Yeta traveled; no passerby's- nada. She dearly thought inside, *"who in the fuck is this person?"*

Being a little nervous, and about sixty paces from the stop, Yeta reached in her backpack and grabbed two solid black .45 caliber handguns so small that they would make a hitman nervous. Without breaking stride, she yanked one in the chamber for both arms and continued to the bus stop. The man seemed not to notice Yeta because he did not move at all, and as she neared the shelter she could see he was not facing her. "If he tries me, *he's mine*," she admitted silently. At age twenty-three, Yeta was an experienced shooter and was not afraid to defend herself… anywhere, it was just something she took very seriously – everyday. At about thirty paces away, the man still did not move his body at all as if it was a mannequin. She paused pace to look around and made sure that no other odd bodies were lingering, she saw nothing. There was no sign of nothing but the sound of early day nature in La Floríd during beautiful Mayo. Yeta sped pace until she was close, then walked right up to the man, guns aimed… *"Who the fuck are you?"* She demanded. Now that she was up close to the man, she noticed that he was of mexican origin, late forties to early fifties, slender build, was wearing all black -a jacket, slacks and dress type shoes- smelled like new leather and most interestingly of all, he had an afro and did not show any fear of her nor her arms.

"Easy, easy," pleaded the man, moving his arms for the first time. "I here to catch train."

"Train?" Asked Yeta, giving the man a lost stare.

"Yes, train...it comes through here soon," said the man with a heavy accent. Yeta was wondering why he wasn't speaking to her in spanish as if he couldn't tell that she herself was mexican. They continued in so called English :

"No fuckin' train comes through here at all. *Who are you*? Can't you tell my guns are loaded?" She responded with heat. The man looked at both guns but did not comment.

"Yes, train stop here...aqui."

"*Can* you see my guns are loaded!?" She asked him slowly, as if he was dumb.

"Please. I need fifty-cents for train. I go back home, to Mexico," responded the man. Yeta about lost it.

"Yo! Can you not hear me?" She stated, waving her guns at the man.

"Fifty-cents please, I no have much time. Mexico train is here soon. Please, young lady," he beseeched. Yeta started a fire inside of herself from being so mad - started to sweat little. For the life of her, she couldn't understand why some strange man was talking about some train, on *her* bus stop, in the middle of the country. Not only is he talking about a train, he's talking about *Mexico*; taking a train to Mexico for *fifty-cents*? In 2018? Is he serious? Yeta knew something was wrong with this guy, but what was it? She didn't feel threatened by him at all. The look in the mans' eyes contained no lie and his body language was sincere to his face.

"Yo, what are you talking about?" She asked the man far beyond all curiosity. "What train, why are you on my bus stop?"

"The Mexico train come here, I lost. I need to get back home, to Mexico," answered the man. As he spoke, the man did not really move his arms much; he seemed rather calm but direct. At this point, Yeta realized that her bus was on its way as well; but why does his train come close to the same time as *her bus*? Why is she even, for lack of better wording, tickling this dead feather? Is dude plotting? Why is he here? Was he following her? All those thoughts, and more, were running through Yetas' wild mind. The time was now 5:42 ante, and she was now getting restless.

"Hey, Jesus…Pedro…or whoever you are -today is Friday- *hoy es Viernes*. I was born on a Friday, I love Friday. Where was you and your train at earlier in the week?" When Yeta finished, the man looked confused in the face.

"I no understand," he replied. "I lost. My train come right here, very soon. Please, fifty-cents, if you have. My train come real soon. See, there," he pointed to what Yeta knew was an empty field.

"Jesus, gotdammit', that's the oldest trick in the book cabron," stated Yeta, without at all looking where the man pointed. "Didn't I tell you I got eight shots a piece in these girls I'm holding? I'm not looking anywhere but at you!" Yeta exclaimed, waving her guns at him, this time activating the red beams.

"Please mam…train. I no mean to anger you. I sorry, fifty-cents mam, please, if you have," he pleaded. The man was not changing his story, nor his body language. Yeta could still see that his eyes were not lying, and not only that; he was innocent, not trying to harm her.

"I can't believe I'm doing this!" Yeta cried aloud as her head started to hurt. She reached in the pocket of her jean shorts and grabbed some of the change she used for her bus fare, sifted through it and found two quarters. "Here's your fifty-cents, muchacho," she said while walking closer to the man. Yeta tossed him his fifty-cents and they landed right in the man's hands as he braced for the catch. Once he possessed those fifty-cents his eyes lit up like he saw raw gold.

"Let me put my guns up, my bus will be here soon, unlike your train," she finished, looking to her east down the quiet road to spot the bus about a half-mile or so away.

"Thank you very, very much!" The man elated. I ask many people for fifty-cents, many people, many ricos melanos; no one give me nothing, *only you*. Thank you, I go back to Mexico now, because of you," finished the man, smiling so hard that his face looked like an oval.

"Yea sure muchacho, don't be here tomorrow," responded Yeta, smiling a little at the man in all seriousness. The time was now 5:48 and the bus pulled to the side of the road, lowering its hydraulics to let Yeta on. Right before she boarded the bus she turned to look at the man one last time – but he was *gone*. "This isn't possible," said Yeta under her breath as her stomach dropped and butterflies came. She looked all around, but there was no sight of the man at all which caused her to become bewildered -staring into space- forgetting about the bus.

"Heyyy, you gettin' on?" Asked the bus driver. Yeta looked at her and said nothing, then looked right back at the bus shelter where the man was standing. "Honey, I gotta' go baby, I'm sure you do too," said the lady. Yeta looked at her for a few seconds and eventually climbed on the bus. She soon realized that the bus driver was Ms. Hargot, a friend she's made from riding the bus over the years.

"I'm so sorry," persuaded Yeta. "But this guy…"

"What guy?" Asked Ms. Hargot.

"This guy I was just talkin' to, he was just right there," Yeta pondered, pointing to the shelter.

"Honey, I didn't see anybody when I pulled up, just you. I saw you moving around a little…"

"Are you serious? He was just right here, a mexican guy. Said he was lost and needed fifty-cents for a train. I thought…"

"A train baby?" Interrupted Ms. Hargot.

"Yes, a train," responded Yeta. "I thought he was kiddin' me or somethin' but he wasn't threatening or intimidating at all."

"A train, at least from what I know, has never came through this part of La Floríd baby, are you alright?"

"Yea, I'm alright. I gave him the fifty-cents, he thanked me. I turned to see how far this bus was down, started counting my change right before you pulled up, looked back to him and he was gone."

"He's gone?" Asked Ms. Hargot, as if she wasn't believing Yeta.

"Yea, he's gone. The man that kept saying he was lost and wanted to go back home, to Mexico."

"You really saw someone baby?"

"Yes -Ms. Hargot- I did...I can't believe that you didn't see him. He looked to be almost fifty years old, had a little afro. He just... disappeared."

"That's like an unsolved mystery, you need to be on a tv show with that story honey. Go ahead and take a seat, this one is on me. We about to get on the freeway in a lil' while so we can get you to work on time," said Ms. Hargot, cautioning for traffic while giving Yeta her transfer ticket.

"Thank youuu!" Yetas' response echoed on the way to her seat in the back. There was never anyone on the first two express buses so Yeta took full advantage of the solitude. Still wrapped in awe of the entire situation regarding the man, she found herself aimlessly staring at the countryside and eventually dozed off. Was she living a dream? Who was the mysterious man? Yeta probably would never know. There was about a twenty-minute ride left before she would arrive by work, giving her much time to sleep off any mind stress she may have had.

"Young ladyyyy!" Declared Ms. Hargot. "We're at your favorite place," she finished, nudging Yeta's shoulder a little. Awakening to see she was at her stop, Yeta rose with her backpack still on.

"Thank you, Ms. Hargot," Yeta said while stretching. "Thank life it's Fridayyy," she slightly yawned.

"That's right honey, we get to sleep in don't we," stated Ms. Hargot.

"Yesss, shit- I'm tired- plus I get paaaid."

"Speakin' of that, when you gonna' start drivin'? I know you tired of being late and catching this dam bus. You got money."

"I don't wanna' spend it tho'. Cars are a headache. That *man* though, I can't shake it off."

"Well try not to think too much about it. Think about that dam car," laughed Ms. Hargot, along with Yeta as she exited the bus. It was about a two-minute walk from the stop to her law office and the time was 6:15, the sun was trying to show off. Regardless of a big pay day, it being another beautiful day in La Floríd, her mothers' south american wedding in two weeks – nothing mattered to her right now but that strange man at the bus stop. He just, appeared then disappeared. Yeta kept her eyes crawling around everywhere, gun in hand, to ensure she wasn't being followed or that no other strange persons were lingering. There were about four different entities housed in a cul-de-sac in the business park where her office was. Young palm trees and thick vegetation saturated the park, making it hard to see clearly in between the businesses. The light from the Emerald gas station quickly faded as Yeta made it to her office. Unlocking her heavy security door, she hurriedly entered the office and grabbed the ak-47 she kept mounted on the entry wall and locked the door behind her. With her .45 docked on her waist, she prowled through each room of her hard-earned building and found no one. Three employees worked at the Gardens Law Office, but all were off today. At age twenty-three, Yeta was a more successful lawyer than anyone in all of Copperton; however, many people were jealous of her which was why she always guarded herself closely, *and she was good at it.* Yeta walked into her office and cranked on her automatic smoothie machine, laying her ak and .45 on her desk. Though she was comfortable with the three-hundred-sixty-degree security system on her wall, Yeta still wondered about the man. *"What the fuck happened to me today?"* She asked herself aloud in between gulps of her strawberry smoothie. Since it was Friday not much work would be done, just counting mail and studying a few of her open cases; relaxing in silence. While working, Yeta found herself constantly wondering about that man, and that train. She started to think hard about the events from earlier and became deeply lost in her imagination: *fifty-cents, Mexico, train; fifty-*

cents, Mexico, train. She couldn't make any sense of it; there was nothing special about her at all, she thought. The opening and closing of car doors outside signified that it must have been close to 8ante, and other businesses were near to open. All Yeta could even think about was *that man*. "I'm just gonna' go," she said to herself. A little progress was made in her studies; hence, she didn't feel wrong by leaving early. Grabbing her backpack and mounting the ak on her office wall, she shut down the master lock, which automatically locks all doors once she exited the front door of the office, activated a red beam to the compact .45 and exited her office, almost blinded by the early bright sun of La Floríd. The time was now 8:15, five minutes before the bus back into the country would arrive. Still monitoring her surroundings, she saw nothing out of the ordinary besides the cicadas racking louder than normal. Yeta surely had correct bus fare but still checked her pockets to make sure, and noticed she had a few extra coins. Upon examination, she found two extra quarters and also noticed that her transfer ticket lasted all day instead of expiring around 8ante as normal.

"This is some strange shit," Yeta said aloud to herself. "Maybe Ms. Hargot looked out, I know she let me on free, maybe I put some extra change in my pocket...am I alive right now?" She asked her internal self. Now at basically empty Pine Boulevard, Yeta crossed with a minor jog and looked west to see the bus was about two stop lights away. For some reason stemming from earlier, Yeta looked behind her just out of reflex expecting to see something interesting but saw nothing. This bus stop didn't have a shelter and was also without a seat. As the bus neared then pulled to the side of the boulevard, it was easy to see that Ms. Hargot was the driver again. The bright red flowers in her locked hair stood out like the sun would at night; not more than her smile though.

"You had you a real short day huh?" Asked Ms. Hargot as she giggled.

"Yes mamm," responded Yeta. "My mind was wandering then I was bored, so home I go." She showed Ms. Hargot her transfer.

"Alright now, thank you honey. Now you think about that car."

"I will, said Yeta, walking to the back of the bus as not many people were riding. This time, Yeta stayed awake the entire ride, gazing at the countryside, deep in thought again about the events from earlier; wondering why it happened and if it had any meaning to or in her life. She's twenty-three years old, no children, successful -whatever the hell successful is- and had no skeletons in her closet. There was one time though that she shot at -but didn't hit, at least from what she knew- a random group of guys for yelling cruel, rude and threatening comments directly towards her while she was on a late-night jog. Now, she never jogs at night, period. Closing in on her stop, Yeta walked carefully to Ms. Hargot as the bus began to slow down.

"Thanks for everything Ms. Hargot. I know you don't believe me, but I really did see a strange man today," said Yeta - pointing to the bus stop across the country road.

"I'm sure you did honey," replied Ms. Hargot. "He ain't there now though," she added. Both women shared a laugh. "Before I retire, you better done had you a car. Two years is a long time to ride a city bus when you don't need to young lady."

"Yes you right, I been thinkin' sometimes …luxury or sport, all black -sickkk."

"You do that, and when you get it, let ya' hair blow in the wiiiind honey," stated Ms. Hargot.

"I will, I'ma do just that, I'll see you later," Yeta said as she exited the bus.

"Later honey," responded Ms. Hargot, closing the bus door and continuing on her way. Since she always made good time on her routes, Ms. Hargot could have little talks with Yeta and never be behind schedule; that's how they became good amigas. It was now 8:40 and the sun was baking. With a ten- minute walk in front of her, Yeta took a deep breath as she crossed La Linda road, staring at the bus stop, immediately flashing back to what happened earlier. That man, that whole situation, especially the train...what train though? Of course, now there was no one at the bus stop and surely no sign of a train. With a clear mind, compared to earlier, Yeta pulled out her phone and researched any train history in her area. The first few pages of her search results brought no useful information worth reading. The fourth page was headed with an interesting link titled: *1851 Ghost Train in Upper La Floríd: Truth or Myth?* Yeta's eyes got real big. She clicked on the desired link with fidgeting hands and it led her to what looked like an antebellum newspaper article from 21 May 1857; the publisher was *The Early Daisy*; Newspaper: *Southstate Gazel*.

    Yeta thought it was just way too convenient for that article to appear, but she read on:

An american man, whose name we won't say, of middle age, of sound mind and competence, with direct attachment to the land said that on Saturday, 21 May 1851, he saw a shadowy figure of a man, not too tall in stature, standing in the middle of a field on his land, not too far from where he was tending corn. We will refer to the american as a farmer for this story; he continued to say he saw the figure pace, rather calmly, back and forth, as if he was awaiting something or someone. The figure never looked toward the farmer.

Yeta couldn't believe what she was reading. She looked around to ensure no one was wondering the lone country roads as she walked home. Seeing nothing, she jumped right back into the article, now on page two:

The farmer drew his hunting rifle he kept on his back- but did not sight at the man- for the man began to stand still, then, from the sky it seemed, he heard what sounded like a train sounding its faint horn, as if it was near. In astonishment and fear both, he looked back at his farm house and surrounding lands and saw nothing, looked to his front and noticed the man was no longer there. The sound of the mysterious train horn was no more. As a credible man known for sharing his surplus yield, the farmer's word is very reliable. There have been no other reports of this story.

After noticing the man was gone, the farmer quit his work and ran to tell his wife of the same age, whom of which also heard the train horn but saw nothing while she looked out of the kitchen window. All of this was said to occur around six-thirty in the early day. He waited three or so hours to share his story with authorities because he felt he would lose his hard-earned earthly credibility. The farmer nor his wife had no other information about the shadowy figure, and since have not saw it nor any other figures.

"What the fuck?!" Yeta emitted. She read the story so fast that she needed to talk to herself for more clarity. *"What is this area I'm in? Who is the farmer, and did he see the same guy I saw?"* This Friday was a good one for Yeta. Now within a few hundred yards of her property, Yeta focused in on making it home and relaxing. Staring at her land which was now in better view, she noticed that some type of vehicle was parked in her driveway. There are no neighbors for at least the equivalent of about four New York city blocks, hence; accidental parking by some lost driver was not a plausible explanation. In addition, she has not many friends who would just drive into the country to see her unannounced. *Something* was wrong. By reflex, Yeta tucked herself behind some brush and took out a pair of her decent binoculars to zoom in on her house and property. She made out a dark, long and rather shiny item as the ride in the driveway, but no one was inside. No matter how closely she studied, she couldn't make out if any breaches were in or around the front and sides of her property and she didn't see any signs of a break-in. "What the fuck is goin' on!?" She uttered continuously. Replacing the binoculars with her pistols, Yeta cautioned through the thick country brush, dirt paths, flies and pockets of gnats on the way to her house, intent on damaging any potential antagonists. About twenty-five yards or so before she reached her driveway, Yeta slowed in her stride, unable to process the object in her eyes. A brand new 2018 Mercedes-Benz was the out of place automobile in question; it was one of those big long ones, which has been of her interests lately- therefore; she knew that car inside and out. *"Who's fuckin' car is this yo?"* She whispered inside of her head. Running up to the automobile Yeta could easily see that it was in pristine condition, clean- no noticeable dirt nor debris on any of the unworn tires nor under carriage. A little hesitant to open any doors, Yeta again looked around to see if anyone was lurking and saw nothing. Taking a deep breath, she opened the drivers' door and saw a red envelope in the center console. "This car smells so new, the leather and plastic smell is so strong that it's taking my breath," she groaned. As she grabbed the envelope and closed the door, she could feel something else besides a card. Out she pulled two keys bearing the Mercedes-Benz emblem. Inside of the solid red card were some ink-written words she never will forget:

Para el cincuenta centavos,

gracias joven...

Por favor, saca el automovil,

ahora es suyos Yeta.

iii

A Mad Society

By way of default - blood drips from a cut, flowing down the arms of the pure and the mutt - started as a bruise from a hidden uppercut, landing on the jaws of the pure and the mutt. Nothing was explained why they couldn't feel pain, looking in the mirror they saw something strange - so very strange it could ruin anything, scary as death it could change everything. Pain they could see in the form of a bruise where was it from and what could they do? Pure as they are - at least so they thought, who was the fault and what was the cause? Following laws - at least so they thought, praying to god - at least so they thought, tithing for good - at least so they thought. Slowly the seekers are finding the faults, learning the truth of against prior thought - knowing somebody is ripping them off...

What guns are for

Creaks on the floorboard wrinkle through the house,
in came a question mark wearing no towel -
naked as a pedophile with a hunters' smile,
searchin' for a fix,
sifting through its snout,
on dead zoom for the catching of a child.

The sadness

If from a show is how you play cards,
you wouldn't recognize you in your front yard!
Words from the wise are in charge to discard
the pale nimrod lurking in your front yard.

Who's in the mirror if you don't know you?
What are you looking at if it's not true?
Answers are hidden in caverns of you,
learning yourself was not taught at school.

You know where it is, it started with you -
before you began it was stolen from you,
put in a box and left on a stoop
for pale milkmen storing milk for a few.

How can it be that you don't know you -
but know everybody in the online stew?
How can it be that you talk to the crew
but don't know self, you never talk to you?

Food for thought!

The end of the beginning

While you watch netflix
said guys make hits,
replacing the water that's under the bridge by
filling the gaps with gaseous mists.

The beginning of the end

Know who they are and remember they scar,
know what to do when they enter your yard.
Written in stone are the pieces apart,
bond them as one with love from your heart.
Nothing is easy and nothing is hard,
life is a movie you must play your part...

¡¡¡Cuidadooooo!!!

¡Oh no!

¡No saca fotos de Macheté -
hiciste pregúntale!?
Sin no -
tú debes a correr
pronto -
como tienes a usar el baño!

Partials from Macheté

I challenge you to challenge me,
in your challenger you couldn't challenge me,
even on the beat, ain't no catchin me -
with the real ain't nobody matchin' me;
it's a tragedy,
in your challenger, you can't challenge me.

Me and you,
one on one I challenge thee -
I can challenge you
but remember you can never challenge me.

All up in ya space, will you challenge me?
It's a tragedy,
in your challenger you couldn't challenge me.
Ain't no catchin' me
you a tragedy,
you will never be,
in your challenger, you can't challenge me.

Pick this apart

The lands they salted,
  bodies in the coffins,
    horror stories written,
      odious authors.

                Those of the Caucus,
      chosen and the authors
      causing all the problems,
      bloods in the waters.

What is surely solvent,
  skin of the fallen -
    ancient in its calling,
      the universal solvent.

These people are real Pokémon

Walking in groups face down in the glue,
following a path unknown to the crew -
smiling like kids on the last day of school,
happy as can be but they seem see through -
longing at a screen for the next new clue,
lost as can be and face down in the glue;

lost as can be and face down in the glue,
lost as can be and face down in the glue.

By 2

The silence of my soul leaves prints in the snow;
prints in the sand, plenty prints on my land -
darts in my heart leave stones on my face,
stones in my veins - many stones in my way.

Knives in my back leave hell in my spine,
hell in my chins - much hell on my mind.

Pains from my life leave hammers at my eyes,
hammers at my knees - hammer me 'til I cry.

Lies to my face leave trust on the floor,
trust on the floor - I trust no more!

Minuscules

My cups, my plates;
my forks, my spoons
my land my state
my sun my moon

my clothes my shoes
my wood my nails
my books my rules
my ship my sail

my cars my trucks
my roads my rails
my grass my mud
no room for snails.

Macheté, the beauty of it all

Mí día es oscuro,
oscuro es mí noche -
mí vida es oscuro y
luz es mí corazón,
soy un hombre oscuro?

Pendejos

Allí, está muchos pendejos -
todas formas y tallas;
aquí no está pendejos
con ropas y zapatos lo mismo -
palabras y frases estupidos,
todos están pendejos.

Don't Include them

As a first in line, don't
share with the folks who
left you dead,
lifeless in the mud.

No matter who it is,
mom dad bro sis,
you got left once so
don't include them.

¡¡¡Pistolas!!!

Mí pistola es mí amiga,
tú no eres mí amiga -
porque un día, estás esa...
un día, estás eso -
mí pistola está lo mismo...

I drink Blood

Where the walls meet is
where my eyes meet,
standing in a corner
searching for mystique,
ravaging my brain full speed
for a treat;
finding where I failed is
oh' so sweet,
helping me to slowly patch
both wounded knees.
In a dark room and
the only light forms are
the bravest of rays that
seared black shades.
Where the walls meet is
where my eyes meet -
standing in a corner
searching for mystique.

De la noche, again bitch

Don't crucify me,
I walk a lone path of
soiled hood streets and uncut grass -
looking to the sky with
crust filled eyes.
I break a blunt down, its
time for some laughs,
taking many drags
until I feel grand,
I see an old broken heart
in my right hand -
and a couple crashed lungs
in my left hand,
gotta' save my fingers
from catching in a fan.

Don't crucify me!
I wear a large smile and
I wear a large frown
so I play the middle ground.
Don't crucify me!
I am not a lad in
tight church pants and
color in my hair.
Don't crucify me!
Shake my bread tree and

I'll blow your head off in
the middle of the street.
I tried so hard
being humble outwardly,
all I got back is denial heartbeat.

Show me what ya' got

Monstrame dos cosas -
Quien estás y donde estás?
Pregunta su madre sin
no tú sabes -
yo quiero a saber
dos cosas:
de donde eres – y
que es en su cabeza...?

(your title goes here)

Usandote a nada -
bebe el sanguine de su rodilla.
Donde yo cortate
y saliote en la calle
sangrando como ladrones
es donde yo estára,
no olvida -
soy yo-me en mí calles.

El Invierno, dos veces

Están muertos
están muertos,
el viento es
saplando loco,
lejos del barrio.

Están muertos
están muertos,
falso en sus vidas,
con nada en sus mochillas -
llevan nada
porque esos mochillas no
es sus mochillas...
están muerte
están muerte,
con nada en la cabeza
y nada por las gentes,
molestá por las gentes
matarles ahora.

están muertos,
están muertos.

En mí palabras

Doble izquierda -
mira a mí enemigo
cara a cara
que vas a decir -
o vas a espigar?

Doble derecho,
puedes a ver la lluvia?
Todos en su dirreción,
detras de lluvia es no sol;
pero es el enemigo con
frequencia, mirando a sacar mí vida.

My disclosure

If volume one was the nail,
volume two is the hammer that
won't need nails - every
word for itself;
none of this work
rhymes like snails,
for you to think, for me
to tell;
to tell the world but not
to sell;
from my heart a fire fell,
through the clouds, down
to earth,
through the rain and through
the ground,
through the core and through
the crown,
through the lost but can't
be found,
heat this deep won't be
put out.

Fear of the unknown

Through my window came
a sea,
one night by a breeze.

One summer night -
in came a beam of
unknown light, source out of sight.
Dark in my might, I
grabbed a steel piece though
I had stage fright,
trembled through the night;
heart in my throat,
legs strong for a flight,
shadows in the dark drained
blood in my heart,
I've trained in the field
but not this part...

...*me against me*...

No Autenticas

Eres aburrido con no partido,
lento como hablas;
pero estás un politico?
Lento como hablas,
tú no haces mucho...
lento como hablas
y caminas muy lento,
está serioso?
No no no,
eres aburrido con no partido.

How is this?

The blanket under trouble is soiled with flesh,
dead as a nail removed from its neck,
under the hat on the head of the gnat
is all dead skin, plastic
for rats.

Grafted explosion

From the devil came a plan
and then a right hook,
there was no pain present
just the hoax of being fooled.

By the time it's figured out,
It can't be overruled,
here came a haymaker,
the result was charter school.
Here came a haymaker
that built the public schools,
lying to our children and
breeding them as fools,
here came a sucker punch
and now you have some rules
you must adhere to
unless you build a school.
We have our school board,
the rest is up to you.

Before bed 2014

A variety of images parade in my brain,
they meet in the middle to form a collage,
molding ideas into concrete block.
I shuffle my cards and deal in my heart
planning plus acting to get in my spot,
if not,
they might throw me from the scaffold
or embarrass me like she who wore the A
or worse,
branding me a slave would take the cake-
active during day-
into darkness I flee.

Hoy es hace calor

Hoy es hace calor!!!

    Someone we all know let they friend run all through they house, nothing was stirring, not even the loud. They took everything- I mean, everything, locked niggas up and took the house-loud ass niggas turnt to a church mouse, scared half to death of never getting back on...they won't regain. Great bitch stories do these niggas sing, knowing the robbers and friends with the accomplices. Wearing a badge of a generous lame, niggas call uncle and will never do a thing. Please brace now for what I'm gon' say: One shorts one some grits on accident, fuck the bullshit- he wants him dead! Over two grits...just a few grits but his friends teamed up and took his shit, laid niggas down and niggas didn't do shit.

Bad weather

Inclimate as it is-
hot and muggy,
cold and frigid,
surviving a storm of
disbelief is not simple.
Minor is the symptom but major the struggle,
should I let her walk,
my coat in the puddle?
She may let me down
just so I can love her?
Then it was cool but
now it just isn't.
Some seem cool then
change to a bitch of
everlasting hell, hot and muggy-
cold and frigid,
surviving a storm of
disbelief is not simple.

Beneath State

Standing midfield on the brinks of a cusp,
pools of standbys waiting for fresh blood.
Waiting for the cue to release bad fumes,
white sandmen meet a hole in their gloom-
black sandmen meet a hole in their gloom,
not do they know they are due for the stew-
so do they think they are better than you.
sent on a mission to watch all you do.

¿Donde estoy?
"Don't worry about it bitch."

Some act like Dolomite with tunnel sight-
livin' lives from a handle out of sight,
swear on the truth but fragile as can be-
eating from mother and eating her trees,
forming new routes for the birds and the bees
spinning a web simply right around me.

If I
blink twice, better yet I blink thrice
my soul taps tight like a pit bull bite.

Very thick skin which will help in a fight
is the relief if I take off for flight!
Meet me in class with a book of your type-
all I will bring are the books that are mine.
Truth from the world always bringeth the fright,
truth comes around and the writers recite-

Time after time niggas claim as a sheik
but don't know shyt, sellin' lies for a fee-

In my own world crafting lines from my seat,
out of the ground are the scripts I complete.

Regurgitation

Never have we been so close to the end,
better have some words with your last few friends-
on the other hand I don't have no friends,
I don't give a dam what the hell brings them.
Surely as can be,
when the walls cave in,
the roof on your house and its halls cave in.

Here come the troops in the ugliest suits,
don't have hearts for the hearts they consume.
Women get raped and the babies get raped,
men get the same bodies thrown in a lake
much was consumed none of it went to waste,
when they want blood it is never in haste.

What's up???

Matter erasers are
eating away...eating away...

away at my brain for doing the same,
doing the same, doing the same-

same every day- a spiritual waste;
doing the same is eating my brain,
eating my brain, eating my brain.

Doing the same is a problem I have-
eating away... eating away...

...away at my brain for doing the same-
doing the same, doing the same.

¿Quien es en?

Probamente los hombres de Rome-
quien quiere a ser blanco;
pero
en publico;
ustds. fingan a ser todo negro y
hablan como negros-
pero,
que hacen eso?
Yo sé uds. trabaja
para el gringo hombre-
no mas no menos!

Galaxies baby, galaxies

If music is a friend then sound is a friend,
noise is a foe who cannot yet blend,

now we have static, starting at the granite,
way to the skies where galaxies inhabit.

Not yet blended,
noise is a foe that pollutes a planet -
yellow in the snow.

Woman is the tone where heartbeats bloom,
growing into sound from the right attitude.

No more noise,
gone with the wind is noise and static,
man from boy.

The last full moon!!!

Who's coming out on the last full moon?
Do we have ghosts or do we have ghouls -
do we have groups or do we have fools -
on the last day we will break all rules,
howl through the town and release dark fumes,
drawing lost souls to be under dark rules.

Who's coming out on the last full moon?
One last feast by the boiling of a stew,
going all out so we have much room,
searching for a plot to resume exumes -
lost loved ones with the sauce for the stew,
maps of the world much before ill grew.

Who's coming out on the last full moon?
Make a small slit on the arm with the broom,
take a small sip of the red brewing you,
now feel the old world deep inside of you.

Who's coming out on the last full moon?
Hell's coming out with intent to recruit.

4 minutes

Can you feel the hate out here?

In and on my ears are
wounded cries,
blood leaking from the rear.

Why am I sad when I feel so strong-
staring at the sky with the same ole song -
"crybaby crybaby,"
where'd I go wrong?

Sleeping with my guns just so I don't fall.

9 minutes

She came in my house and left her skit
as a bouquet of her own flower scent --
gave me a bath in some petals of her sense,
cleansing my pores with her method to heal
like a vapor rub to relinquish all sin,
she who watches me is the key to my skin,
easing my mind with her handiest quilts.

What is up?

With all the black shootings -
all the black killings,
if black lives matter then
why are they doing?
Preachers give peace but
why are they lying?

Black lives matter ran
by a white guy -
so black lives matter?
Why are you crying?
I feel much blacks even
though I'm not black
the blacks hate me,

what is up with that?

I just don't know why

Why set me up for a hardcore fail?
Big wide eyes on my face play fair -
on the battlefield with your shirt tucked in,
for the white house do you wear that pin -
for a small check do you chastise friends,
dear do you hold what the pale guy did -
gave you a chance to evade death beds,
one false move and you lose both hands.
Not just friends but you chastise fam,
chastise mom and you chastise dad -
love don't matter in the pale homestead,
one false move and you get pushed down -
off at the knee then you fall to the ground,
he who you praise is nailing you down,
all of your work and all of your clout -
gone with a blink and will not be found.

Running on

The danger of a so-called slave from Songhay is so unreal for a present day boy who looks like you but was told by a few good men that he was African and not American, at all; but they wonder why the boy falls. Wonder why he's sad and wonder why he has no help from the law - not from highway men nor police as they're called who bring no help just bring no help but deep inside they will kill if it helps the large in charge but small at heart. The few good men who told the boy he was a slave from Songhay are well informed the boy was not, to keep their pay they fuel the plot.

En Sanguine

Sangrando de mí ojos,
baja mí cara,
sangrando de mí orejas,
baja mí cara.
Sangrando de mí nariz,
baja mí boca
baja mí cuello,
baja mí cuerpo,
a la piso...
baja mí pies.

Last Quarter of 2016

So many killings -
	innocent of guilt,
So many dying -
	patches on the quilt.
So many crying,
	splinters in their skin -
So many plotting,
	serial with filth -
So many lying -
	knuckles on the lips.
So many staining,
	cavities in hills.

So many changing,
	everyday a new...
So many losing
	even with the spoon.

Halloween; a De la noche story

Parade around in blackface in a sackrace,
one dark knight followed by a moon face,
all black down with an arm and a cape,
joker face grin and the red cupcakes,
buddy won't budge if the strap holds eight -
all heads turn when you see blackface,
one dark knight followed by a moon face,
out for the cheese in a sole rat race.

Parade around in blackface in a sackrace,
one dark night followed by a moon face -
off with your head if you don't play safe,
joker face grin and the red cupcakes.

Parade around in blackface in a sackrace,
one dark knight followed by a moon face.

Intrusion

Splinters in the floor pinch through new socks,
wake up calls vibrate from the docks of
men by ship who control all clocks
tracing soundwaves from your lifelong cough.

Oye!

Que pasa?
No pone manos en
mí ensalada,
o en mí galletas!
Estás un novato,
en mí mochilla está pistolas
no tacos,
soy peligroso vato y tu?
Tú digas tú tambien,
eso no cierto -
dame todos su nachos-
ahora no manana.

Who in the world are you people?

Who am I walking into
a trap with –
runnin' the streets of
cold insolvence;
same color skin but
play with the cards gave
by the same men
looking to sink ship and
crush to death those
they ran to live with,
running from those they
couldn't live with.

Eyes on the stars

Closer and closer
the bells the bells.
Further and further
the spells the spells.
Sooner and sooner
the quells the quells,
now and forever
the bells the bells.

The Riddler

They can nothing you until
they run out of nothing,
you fight for nothing and
it shows nothing was nothing –
day one they had nothing,
everytime you speak it as
if it was something,
now they have a title
created out of nothing.

Elegant Acts

Full of an ass
lookin' for the ass to
fuck another ass and
watch the ass leak...
raping the strong,
the lost and the weak.

Brazen Scientifics

Brazen on the skin of the
well known man are
unknown years of the
soul from the sand.

Right on the chin of the
well known thief is
sperm from the man he
forced under siege.

In between the legs of the
so-called tramp
is well known life that
grew most out.

The wrong ones

blood down the face of the unknown man...
as a small spring that first was a hole
from a handgun in the right mans hand
came to be a hole that had to grow
from a strong blow from the right hand man
onlookers know what they did not know

You should just keep walking

I can't and won't be bought
it ought not come with costs
while moving pass the sloth
all through the parking lot
right past the barber shop
just past the nail salon
there is the naked truth
forgot its haltertop
you see the naked truth
and still you wonder not

I can't and won't be bought
it out not come with costs
with that team I don't rock
because I am a rock
I mean no disrespect
but I call all my shots
you chose to be with them
I surely chose to not
you chose to be with them
and them you question not

I can't and won't be bought
it ought not come with costs
all through my underworld
into my overworld

there cannot be a fault
because I am the boss
it came into my hand
away I chose to toss
it came back to my hand
and built itself a post
I can't and won't be bought
it ought not come with costs

It happened *so* fast

"You must deposit the check no later than 11 p.m. in order for the full amount to become available to you on the next business day. Please withdraw full amount and secure safely. Ensure that you remain calm and act normal. The bank teller is aware of this act but is unable to tell much until it is too late. Once you are secure and away from any undesirables, notify the courier at the number provided below. Please remain discreet. You will receive your 10% of the amount within 3 days after today. Please provide the courier with a location to drop off your 10%.

If you have any questions, please respond to this email.

Thank you

Human Resources

"Hey man, *what the hell is this*?" Asked David's best friend Brad. "Why did you have me read this?"

"Dude, it's the chance I've been wanting for a long time, a fucking cake walk for five-g's," eagerly responded David, smiling sadistically.

"Bro, are you still on that lost web shit bro? I thought you were done with that. It's like two weeks until Alpine; our own dorm bro, chicks, pizza. Get a grip dude, bad play," replied Brad.

"Brad, this is not fucking football, ok? Bro like, this is big. Yes, I'm still on the deep web, *it's fucking lit*. I'll have five-g's without fucking lifting a finger!" David exaggerated. Both being nineteen now, Brad and David were nearing their freshman year at Alpine State college. Brad, both brains and braun, was a jock in high school and was very popular; David wa the more introverted but minimally social type, he's just too busy trying to take shortcuts through life and looks at too much narcissism on the tube. Even as a jock, Brad still kept his grades up, and David, on the other hand, has copied work from Brad for the past two years; oddest of all, he was a decent student but prefers to cheat, that's just David. Living in the same neighborhood, the duo has been tight since childhood.

"Are you not alive right now, orrr?" David sarcastically asked his friend. "There's a check attached to that email. I'll print it out, sign it, take it to my bank, deposit...bingo!"

"No bingo!" Brad exclaimed. "What the fuck are you doing bro, you think that's gonna' work? You're insane!" Not paying attention to Brad, David walked to the computer where he was sitting, took the mouse and pointed to the paperclip icon in the email, Brads eyes followed. "I'm not opening that attachment, no way" he frantically said, walking out of the computer room.

"Get your panties outta' bunch," teased David. "I'm printing this before my mom comes home." The sound of the printer going on made Brad draw up a bit. He couldn't believe what his best friend was doing, seriously. All the times that David complained about being broke before college have finally culminated into this. Shit, he should have gotten a *gotdam* job.

"So, like...where do you get the five-g's from bro? The email said that the courier's the one paying you, so who is it?" Brad finished.

"Bro, the courier is totally fucking cool. I've already spoken to him bro, he sounds so lit, he's just waiting for me to move."

"Waiting on you to move? Lit? Bro...you said you saw this on the lost web right? What makes you think this is safe, or that they don't know who you are? What the fuck!" Brad finished his rant by closing the laptop screen.

"Whatever dude, I'm holding five-g's right now, right here. Which bank shall I go to huh? Hmmm...ahhh yes, the People's Bank, my bank. Yea boy!"

"Did you tell them that you had that bank? Bro didn't you have to pay with *slotcoin* to even access the site?"

"No duh man," responded David. "I use Safepace, all safe."

"You're making a mistake bro, big time. Let's go outside and get some fresh air," Brad offered.

"You get some fresh air, I'm good. Quick cash is on my mind. I'm trying to get rich dude, gotta' start small," David said sarcastically while texting on his smartphone. What Brad failed to realize was that David was very serious about quick cash. There was no way that David was not going to deposit that check and attempt to enjoy the proceeds, in his little ponzi-scheme imaginary world. It didn't make sense to Brad that David could just withdraw five-thousand dollars from his account when he has never even had that much. "Only time will tell," is how Brad began to feel as he walked outside. He didn't understand David's attachment to the lost web, nor why he travels through it at all. One time, about two years ago, David got into an argument with someone in one of those chatrooms and subsequently and abruptly closed his laptop. A few days later, on Halloween, David's house was egg'd and someone left feces on the front porch and set it on fire. His mother went crazy and poured her idea of Holy Water, which was filtered rain water, all over the porch. Deep inside, David knew exactly why it happened but didn't admit it to anyone.

"Bro I'm out for now bro," Brad announced as he came back in from outside. "Mom needs help with something and she wouldn't say. Bri is at cheer practice," he explained.

"Alright dude, I'll hit you up when I get back from the bank, straight?" Asked David.

"Straight," agreed Brad as they engaged in their buddy handshake. Right when Brad walked out of the room and eventually out of the house, David was already signing the check. He grabbed his keys and left the house as well, smiling. The People's bank was about a ten-minute drive from his mother's house and David was anxious to get this over with, he could just taste those five-g's he thought he would have and what he would do with it: *invest in slotcoin...buying a lot of spice and get high out of his mind before freshman year.* He started his hatchback and slowly backed out of the driveway onto the street, headed straight for the bank. The check of his dreams was safely tucked in his flat wallet. *"This is it,"* he thought to himself. Nearing the stop sign in his Dove Meadows neighborhood, David saw a navy black sedan roll past his view as he haulted at the sign. "Prolly the narcs, I bet fucking Jimmy got busted; spoiled rich kid," he said aloud to himself as the car made a right turn down another block. Apparently, David's use of certain terms indicated that he watched too many urban films. Making his way through a maze of different neighborhoods, after school children and their terrible bus drivers and all types of grandma's driving as slow as possible, David finally pulled up to his bank, which was at the opposite end of Dove Meadows. Only one car was parked outside of the bank, which meant that David would be in and out quicker then he thought.

"Hiii, how are you?" Welcomed one of the female tellers that David didn't recognize; but then again, he never really came into the bank often, he didn't have money of his own.

"Hey, I'm great," responded David, walking over to the red head to see her name was Tula.

"What can I do ya' for?" She asked happily with a large smile.

"I just want to deposit this today," David responded, nervously sliding his signed check under the security glass.

"Ok, let's see what we have here...oh, payroll huh? Cool, let's get this in," said Tula. David was confused at this point, he didn't even look at the check at all, just signed the back of it; he had no idea what it said, who it was written to, nothing, he just...signed it with his *real* name.

"Yea, a side gig," he muttered. "Stocks and stuff, with my Uncle."

"Well, I need one of those type of side gigs myself," giggled Tula. "How did you want this back?"

"Uhhh, I didn't think any would be ready today," David said, still confused.

"It says this," Tula beckoned. She wrote down two numbers on a sticky note and slid it to David. On the note, five-thousand was ready and five-thousand was on hold until tomorrow. David smiled hard on the inside and started immediately thinking about spice and all types of bafoonery, hungry to touch the so-called money he's always been waiting for. His eyes grew noticeably wide and he knew Tula could see it. Before she could even comment, David blurted out...

"Oh, so he paid me what he owes me from tax season, cool. Let me do the whole five for now." Though he answered confidently, David now realized that Tula didn't even ask to see identification, social, nothing. The email sent from the Human Resources department did indicate that the teller won't notice anything, that must have been true.

"Here ya' go, all there for ya' " energized Tula. Under the mirror she slid him five-g's of cold quick cash. David stuttered in his actions but slowly pulled the five g's close to him and he saw Tula smile from ear to ear. Her plain sinister grin caused David to feel cold chills wither around his soul.

"Thank you," he smiled, feeding off Tula's sick grin. "Have a good day," he finished, tucking the two envelopes in his front pockets, one in each. The very moment David stepped out of the bank his cell phone began to go off, but he paid it no attention, letting it ring to voicemail. Once he got into and started his car, the phone rang again. Figuring it was his mother, David answered this time to quickly find out he was sadly mistaking, it was the courier.

"Hey David...what's up man?" Asked the courier, in a hang-ten surfer dude type of voice. Since David spoke to him for almost five minutes earlier in the day, and knowing of the task at hand, he felt no problem or thought nothing odd about the call, but David never gave him his real number.

"Hey dude," uttered David in vagueness while turning right onto Hithalia street. "We're good, I just left the bank bro, we're good. Easier than I thought," he admitted, but said nothing about the strange interaction with Tula. Maybe she was just flirting with him because she saw a ten-thousand-dollar check, who knows. David was so deep in thought about Tula that he forgot he was on the phone.

"Heyy, you still there man...?" Wondered the surfer dude. "Did you hear what I said?"

"Oh shit, yea man, my bad I'm here, my connection was bad. You're clear now, go ahead."

"No worries man. Alright, here's what you do. Take the third left from the bank at Millroad, then stay straight head for two blocks- from that stop-sign, you'll see a dark colored car` on your right, about ten or so houses down the second block that you come to, pull over behind that car cool?" Asked the courier. David was mind-blown that the courier had an idea as to where he was. There were four branches of the People's Bank in Dove Meadows, how would the courier even be remotely close to guessing where he was?

"Uhh ye-yea," David couldn't help but to stutter. "I'm game bro, I'll be there in about five."

"Cool, see ya' then. Thanks bro." The courier sounded upbeat and with those words the call ended. David placed both of his hands on the steering wheel and made a weak left onto Millroad Avenue. It was almost as if his power-steering went out, but the truth was that David was very scared, he had no idea what was going on. The loud ringtone of his smartphone made him almost jump out of his seat. He looked over at his phone on the passenger seat and saw it was Brad calling and he let it catch voicemail. He didn't have time to talk but would call Brad back later when he was done with the strangers he met on the lost web. Gaining strength back in his arms, David gripped the steering wheel tight as he came to the first street, La Playa. "One more block to go," he thought to himself. As he drove through that block, he focused his eyes on the right side of the next block and could see what looked like the car the courier described. "Here we fucking gooo. I can do this, I can do this," he coached to himself, developing more nervousness each second. Now through Bey Lotia terrace and onto the final block, David could see that he was right about what he saw a few moments ago as he saw an arm waving at him out of the dark car; apparently, it was the courier, signifying that he was at the right place. David pulled slowly behind the sedan and the mysterious arm went back into the car, out came the courier. The surfer dude type of image that David developed of this guy quickly faded away as a very tall and muscular man started towards the passenger side of his car. He looked to be of North-European descent, about thirty something-years old and wore a serious face. His dark buzz-cut was serious, he was wearing a black muscle shirt, blue jeans and what looked like hiker boots. David lost fear but began to feel an eminent threat as the man got to the car.

"What's up dude?" Said the courier, leaning into the hatchback. "You got that?"

David felt lethargic, like he had a large rock in his throat.

"Y-yea, five-g's right here," David chattered, barely; holding up the five-thousand in cold cash.

"Good stuff, alright I'll take that," smiled the courier as he grabbed both envelopes. "Now you're coming with us," he grinned, looking at David like he wanted to kiss him. With that said, David couldn't even respond, he was frozen in fear, eye to eye with the courier. Couldn't he just back up then smash down the street to his escape? Before he could get any words out or attempt to flee, in his rearview mirror he saw a black van pull in behind him. To make matters worse, another van pulled up on his left, essentially blocking him in. "Alright dude, the gig is up," ordered the evil looking courier.

"Dude, whhh-wh-wh-what are you talking about Bro? I did what you asked man, I don't need a cut, It's cool," stuttered David in chest choking, obvious fear. He had no idea what was going on, but surely, he fucked up this time; surrounded by strangers – lost web strangers.

"I know it's cool huh, but we can't let you go guy, we just can't. Welcome to the lost web!" With that exclamation, he hit David right above the right cheek and knocked him out cold, slumped in the driver's seat. Out hopped two masked men from the sliding door of the van along the left side of David's hatchback. They threw him into the van, his car still running, while the courier slowly pulled off in his own car, then they followed. The van behind David began to tail the van where David was stored, in a caravan of sickness. It all just happened so fast...too fast; in broad daylight and nobody was around to see anything...or were they? From the house that David was parked in front of came an old lady. At a house directly across the street sat an old man disguised by the column of his front porch, holding a long barrel shotgun. The old lady walked through her yard and got into David's running car, throwing the "OK" sign up at the man who sat across the street and he walked back into his house. She drove his car around the block and parked it in her automatic garage like nothing happened. What David would never know was that the entire side of Dove Meadows that he was banking at was on the take, they were deep in bed with the administrators of the lost web. Specifically, the families in that area *of* Dove Meadows were the minions used to surveil all of the lost web accounts that were created by people not involved with those families. David's side of town, which was Tinselbrook, was just in reach of the dastardly administrators. Being hungry for fast cash, David advertised himself in the infamous "Clear Room" chat with the screenname *Quickdick:* someone down to do whatever to become a backstage member of the lost web VIP server. He was quickly approached by an administrator who forwarded him to the courier which led to the whole fake check deal via email. For one, ten-percent of ten-thousand is not five-thousand, every day of the week it is one-thousand, therefore;

David's math was fucked straight up, Brad didn't even see the check. It was all set up so quick that David was a large sitting duck waiting to be harvested. Once he left the bank, Tula texted the courier and told him the check was cashed which was why David got that call. The lady that took his running car was Tula's mother; the old man with the long shotgun was Tula's father; the courier, Tula's brother. These people were the real team and they did not play games at all for they knew of the great famine.

As the van that stole David climbed on the expressway on its way to the nearest town called Milo Creek, he was still out cold as ever. His smartphone rang loudly and one of the masked marauders pulled the phone from David's pocket to see that it was his mother calling because the screen simply displayed, "MOM."

"Helloooooo?" Asked the thief, cheerfully.

"Um, David stop it, I'm calling to see if you want some Chinese, I don't feel like cooking tonight," explained his mom Carla, as if everything was normal.

"Uhhh, this isn't exactly David," grunted the thief before clearing his throat. Ms. Carla was a little thrown off because she didn't recognize the voice at all and the only person to ever answer David's' phone other than himself was Brad, and this so-called person was not Brad, or was it?

"Brad?" she hoped. "Is this you?"

"Listen mam, David is ok now, we have him and you'll never see him again. This is called random collection the easiest way..."

...*CALL ENDED...*

The Real Mafia, by Macheté

What you see and hear is wrong,
on the screen or in the songs,
such and such in suits or thrones
truly have not been here long,
in the form they don't belong –
but you think they run the streets or
run the screws of industry,
forcing hands to sing along,
but they haven't been here long –
how could they be ancestry?

You forgot your ancestry.

Everlasting

Don't let your hate show,
it'll cost your life.
Keep it to yourself,
you know you don't bite.
Feel the way you wanna –
but keep it in your house,
when you enter public
do not let it out…

…keep it to yourself.

Excerpts

Stretch you out like the last piece of bread in this bitch, smacking gums like granny, let me get my switch – let me get those many acres and a field of pine for my three sets of eyes in this bitch. Look me in those same eyes and you see a dark field, same size as a world crop for whatever yield. Give me all my space back, for you couldn't give any love from those dead crops for whatever yield; you won't see me taking blue nor the red pill – creeping thru a dark night for whatever yield.

El fin!

To the reader

-You have reached the end-

    I would like to thank anyone who has made it this far. Not sure of what you may be thinking after reading this collection; but just know that I had to do it and you made it through the fire – I know I brought the heat! You maintained. I am in great appreciation of you.

All artists need an audience.

macheté,

8 February 2018
3:00 prime

Where to go from here?

     Well, I'm not clear as to where people are going, but I can say that I'm going to *keep* writin', keep imaginin', keep thinkin- growing on a continuum.
     If you at all enjoyed this collection- look for my third volume of this topographical conversation:

Before the early days

Do you have a topographical map of your life conversation??

If **yes**, please draw below.

If **no**, start thinking!

These are some of my sayings

"I am my own competition." 2003

"Everyone has a billboard for the day."
18 October 2015, 8:48 prime

"You would have to have a telescope to score my high jump."
19 November 2015, 8:26 prime

"I'll always have similar sets of eyes on me."
20 February 2016, 7:35 prime

"I'm the type of crop that grows all year 'round."
17 August 2016, 8:37 prime

"Ain't got no money fa ya kids but you buying a grit?"
14 October 2016, 8:37 prime

"Don't think that, at all times, something is not standing next to you that you can't see."
7 November 2016, 5:47 prime.

"I do not consent to stand as surety."
10 January 2016, 6:27 ante

"People's eyes are small."
11 January 2016, 6:32 ante

"Get down to the stone, chards and splinters of the brick, glass and wood that makes the house."
18 January 2017, 4:40 ante

"I can't be defined I can only be described."
19 January 2017, 7:52 ante

"I can like you by the end of a sentence and start hating you by the end."
18 February 2017, 1:26 ante

"Text yourself, love yourself."
15 March 2017, 8:51 ante

"I'm one of those niggas lookin' through garbage for materials, not for foods."
5 April 2017, 6:31 ante

"Eye see you."
5 April 2017, 4:19 prime

"If one doesn't know how to approach, then one should sit back and not approach."
28 April 2017, 9:10 ante

"I'm able to grow wherever I go."
5 June 2017, 8:22 prime

"Now I gotta' come and wake you up before ya' alarm go off." 28 September 2017

"If you walked in the wrong house, nobody would even notice 'cause a lot you niggas look the same." 4 October 2017

"You look like a shelved item, amongst numerous of the same item shelved right behind it." 10 October 2017

"Never in the history of the world has a nigga ever felt very comfortable lookin' like another nigga, until now." 29 October 2017

"Your innertube is filled with shyt, looks like you won't be ridin' that bike."
26 November 2017

"You yourself are and you yourself are in the gold mine, but they tell you that you have to pay to have gold mined? Yea right."
26 November 2017

"This shyt is still a caste system."
9 February 2018.

10 Interesting facts about me

1) I am the true Macheté

2) When I was about 14-15 years young, my internal-self spoke to me and said, "I don't want people to recognize me for my athletic ability." Not many people knew that I played sports ("Alright? SO what do you want?" Was my question/response to myself.) "I want them to recognize me for my brain," was my response. I have no idea where that came from, surely not from anyone else. Even though my life has been kinda' hard because of that, it's all good.

3) I love to communicate. I used to reach out to people to see what they doin', just outta nowhere…it's a part of who I am; however, 95 or more % of the people and so-called family that I've met are fake or close to it. To all the people who I am cordial with, met at a job or in the street, school, wherever - I mean no offense. To the people I used to be real cool with, if we haven't spoken in over two weeks, especially in today's world, we will probably never speak again. Things are different now. Luego!

4) My heart goes out to the good elders and the children.

5) I don't love fiat. I feel like I'm from another time, like the 1700's for example. I feel old, ancient. I have old ways. Very old.

6) I fell out of a tree a looooong time ago, from over ten feet up, man I just laid there. Never seen so much sky in my life. I have no idea what happened after that.

7) I taught myself basic Spanish a lil' bit. I can write and read it a lil', I'm decent.

8) I've always knew that I am not black, nor African-American. Something in myself told myself when I was around 16 years of age. I later found out that I was more than accurate. Soy americano, cierto.

9) I owe myself to myself.

10) I have my own mind, body, and soul, as me myself.

To those I have studied, all by myself...

    I have to say that your work is highly respected here. Thank you for presenting yourself and your diligent research.

I can't say enough!

Gracias,

macheté

macheté

www.ingramcontent.com/pod-product-compliance
Lightning Source LLC
Chambersburg PA
CBHW020848090426
42736CB00008B/282